Books by Susan Day:

Who Your Friends Are
The Roads They Travelled
Hollin Clough
Back
Watershed

Watershed

Susan Day

Leaping Boy Publications

Published by Leaping Boy Publications
partners@neallscott.co.uk
www.leapingboy.com

Diagrams and cover design by Ken Rutter.
The cover image is of the CLOB stone (centre line
of old bank), which still marks the end of the
original Dale Dyke Dam in Loxley valley.

A CIP catalogue record for this title is available
from the British Library.

ISBN 978-1-9998401-6-7

Watershed
1. The region draining into a river system
2. A critical turning point that marks a change

Dearly, **Pauline June**, on 2nd December
following an accident.

Much loved sister of James, Edward, Maureen,
Barbara, Alan, Pamela and the late Vincent,
mother of Heidi and adored Granma of
Jordan, Jarvis, Cassidy and Jayden.

Sheffield Star Friday 8th December 2006

It was an extreme event that happened. It was a bomb, or a shot, or a thunderbolt. It was a giant's axe – no, a cleaver – that came down and cleaved me in two, from the mid-point of my skull, downwards, and left me severed, one part lifeless, the other just twitching, in pain, barely alive.

And then Christmas came anyway.

It comes back to me clearer than yesterday. More than twelve years have passed and I can still remember – I can *see* and *smell* and *feel* – that Christmas Day, imbued as it was, coloured as it was by the overarching pain of what had happened a few weeks before. And even these days, with all that's going on, worldwide disruption, state of emergency, imminent lockdown of entire population – these days will never have the charge, the shudder, the vividness of that Christmas and the days before it and after it, because things come and things go in the world, wars, disasters, earthquakes, they come, they disrupt and shock, they go into the history books. They are elsewhere. They are far away, they concern other people, they are nothing to do with me, I can continue living in my usual way.

Trust me, I was a history teacher – if the World Wars, if the Black Death, if the employment of children as chimney sweeps, if any of that was immediate and personal we would all go around in a chronic state of hopeless distress and sorrow. A class of thirty children could not, at the end of the lesson, get up and put their chairs tidily under their desks (I wish) and go calmly (!) to Maths or PE if the bombing of Hiroshima was something that *really* touched them. I could not have gone coldly to the staffroom for my break time coffee and calmly discussed the need to order more exercise books, or the interesting pairing off of two of my colleagues.

I was a history teacher and now I am a retired old woman, and soon I might be a prisoner in my own home – not even *my* own home, in my view – so as to avoid the virus. We are told there's a virus and we have to believe it, even though the evidence is not in front of our own eyes, only in newspapers and on the TV and radio. And, doubtless, all over the internet, but not there, in front of us, live. And it's like they say: a million Chinese can die and it's something to read in the paper, hear on the TV, and pass over. One person dies, a person you know slightly, a friend of a friend, say, or someone who lives along the street, and it's something to pause over; you might send a card. Someone you know dies, one of your extended family, then yes, you are sorry, you are sad, it leaves a gap. But, that, that thing that happened in December 2006, that changed everything, me, my life, my whole existence. I'm remembering what it was like, I'm writing it down, some of it, writing it down and I could not if anyone was to ask, I could not explain what is the purpose of what I'm doing.

So, official guidance: everything has to shut down for the time being. I went to choir yesterday, my only outing most weeks; not more than half of the normal number of people was there, and the decision was taken to suspend meeting for the foreseeable future. And today the government have officially said the same thing: for the time being there is a prohibition against gatherings of people.

However. I get in my car and drive to the next street to pick up Jojo. I do this three mornings a week – pick him up from home and take him down to Hillsborough to his placement. Nearly every time I go in and spend the morning there, being a bit useful, helping a bit, with Jojo, or with the other service users. (Dreadful term I know, but what is a better one?) The manager meets me at the door – they have been spraying our hands on arrival for over a week now – and tells me she is sorry but now the guidance says I am only allowed to drop him off at the door and watch him be met and have his hands sprayed with sanitizer before he goes in. Are they protecting me, or their service users? I don't know and maybe neither do they.

'We may have to close altogether,' she says. She sees the look on my face and says, 'I know.'

They go on – the press and the media I mean – about this being the worst emergency since the flu epidemic of 1918. That old forgotten bit of history, tacked on the end of a documentary about the First World War. These days history-in-the-making is visiting us, *us* who believed that we had the right to safety and plenty and freedom. Well, freedom if you didn't look too closely. A once in a century epidemic, a virus that can kill anyone – though mostly, they say, old people. Thanks.

People – Heidi's Adam for example – are blustering hopefully that there's nothing to worry about, it's only like the flu, only people who are already ill with something serious have any cause to worry. Other people are anxious; children are scared; there is panic buying. We are being told, over and over, to wash our hands. Over and over. The shops are running out of hand-sanitizer; before this I didn't even know there was such a thing. People are making their own, someone says, from vodka and vinegar.

People are stranded on cruise ships, people are stranded in foreign airports; people who have symptoms must not go out. Their families must not go out. What are the symptoms? Could be anything, varies from person to person – where's a distinctive rash when you need one? Dry cough, temperature – or maybe you can be symptom-free but still infect other people. We are all in the dark, these days.

It came through a blur, Christmas that year, 2006, the weather wet and misty, the lights struggling through the haze. People sent me cards, they came sliding through the front door, making me jump; Christmas cards from people who didn't know, more subdued and dutiful cards from those who did.

Heidi wanted me to go there for Christmas Day – worse, to sleep over there on Christmas Eve, 'So you can see the children opening their presents.' Nothing could be less appealing to me. I wanted to stay at home, on my own, in silence, and not have to give any thought to anyone else. But Heidi wouldn't have it. 'I can't let you do that,' she said. 'It's not what Mum would have wanted.'

'What about what *I* want,' I said.

'I need your help,' she said.

'You've got Gavin,' I said.

'I know,' she said, and simpered a bit, as if she cared deeply for Gavin, though I was pretty sure she didn't. I didn't want her to. 'But still –'

Of course she was in a state. She had every right to be, but so did I. They made me angry, Heidi, her new boyfriend, my brothers and sisters, everybody who seemed to believe that I would be just fine and it was Heidi who needed all the sympathy and all the looking after. They cited the fact that she had four children as a reason why she needed to be especially cared about, where actually the opposite should be true, and the four children would help her get through it with sheer busy-ness. I however had no distractions.

'And anyway,' she said, 'it isn't as if you've got anyone else to spend Christmas with.' Which was true

But I had never *stayed* – or wanted to – at her house, Christmas Eve or any other time and I had no understanding of why she would want me to this time. But after I'd said no several times, giving perfectly good reasons and offering to come early on Christmas morning, she started snivelling and I gave in, as she knew I would. So I went, as late in the evening as I reasonably could, which, however was not late enough that I didn't have to join in with the filling of stockings and the tiptoeing round to put them at the end of beds. The baby was asleep and anyway, too young to have an idea of what was going on. The little girl was asleep too and wasn't disturbed by Gavin creeping about – creeping was a good word for him – being bloody Santa. In the boys' room, so Heidi reported, Jojo was fast asleep and Jarvis was at least pretending to be.

'We can have a drink now,' she said, though from the bottles on the mantelpiece I could surmise that it would not be their first. 'Gin and tonic?' she said to me.

I should have refused it but I didn't, and before I reached the bottom of the glass I could feel myself starting.

'Have another one,' she said but I had just enough sense to stop there. I swiped at my eyes with my sleeve and blew my nose on a tissue and muttered something about having a cold. I think I got away with it.

'I'll get off to bed,' I said. I was sharing Cassie's room, sharing her bed as it turned out which I had not expected.

'She's only little,' said Heidi. 'You'll have plenty of room.'

So I spent a disturbed night in a child's bed interrupted by the dog. It had managed to get out of the kitchen and came up the stairs to whine mournfully and scratch at the boys' bedroom door. Also the baby woke and cried several times during the night and the girl kicked me and coughed intermittently and then bounced out of bed unreasonably early. By seven o'clock they were all up, the stockings had been torn through, there was paper everywhere and Cassie was agitating for the presents under the tree.

'Breakfast first,' said Heidi, and the children began to shovel their way through bowls of sugary cereal while Heidi put the oven on and stood looking forlorn and puzzled at the large turkey.

'Do you know how to do this?' she asked me, but she should have known that I would have no more idea than she did how to cook a Christmas dinner. Neither of us had ever had to do it.

'I can't believe you don't know how to do it,' said Gavin. 'Both of you. I thought anyone could cook a Christmas dinner.' Any woman, he clearly meant. 'I'll ask my mum, she'll tell you what to do.' He took out his phone, a flashy and surely unnecessary gadget, but the mention of the word mum made Heidi start to cry and he put it away again.

I refused breakfast and went to stand in the cold garden with a cigarette, preparing myself to sit through a morning of people ripping paper to fragments in order to get at meretricious bits of plastic and gadgets and ornaments, while working their way through a selection box – the children – and sloshing down Prosecco – Heidi and Gavin. And me probably though I knew it would be a bad idea.

By half past nine I was standing in Heidi's hall face to face – or face to chest – with Gavin. He was big, bearish. Boorish. Not very bright, which was not unusual with her men.

'It's not her fault,' he said. No he didn't say, that would have been halfway civilised. He whined in a grumbling sort of way.

'Funny,' I said. 'To hear you talk this morning, it seems like everything's her fault. Now all of a sudden you're on her side.'

'You can keep your nose out of our business,' he said.

'Look,' I said, 'all I said was –'

'You said you couldn't stand it another minute. You inferred that Heidi's kids were out of order when –'

'Implied,' I said. 'It's you doing the inferring.'

'– it's not their fault either is it? They can't help it if their nannan's passed. Heidi's lost her mum, she don't need any comments from you.'

He adjusted his face to try and look sad. From the front room came the sound of The Snowman on television and of the little girl testing her new toys to destruction, and the buzzes and beeps of some Playstation game. Also of Jojo, muttering in his usual way, with the occasional squeak of excitement or protest.

'Granma,' I said. 'She was not Nannan, as you well know.'

'Whatever,' he said, and gave up trying to have an appropriate expression.

He was, I thought, the most unpleasant ever of Heidi's men. I could smell him, a sort of sweaty smell, overlaid with aftershave and whisky from the evening before. 'You smell of drink,' I said.

'You smell of fags,' he said, and laughed, as if he had won.

I had no more to say. I turned and took my coat – it was on the floor, having been muscled off the hook by Gavin's big work jacket. My handbag was there too, mixed in with assorted trainers and gloves and plastic carrier bags. I picked it up and went out. I had left my overnight bag in Cassie's bedroom, and my toothbrush in the bathroom, and I didn't care at all. He saw what I was doing and started on excusing himself, he's only thinking of Heidi, only wants her to have a nice Christmas, only comes once a year, all that sort of thing.

I went outside and sat in my car in the street. The day was calm and quiet and overcast and there was nobody about. If it weren't for the Christmas trees in all the front windows you'd think it was just any other day.

I sat in my car for some time. I truly intended to go straight home, I truly was not waiting for anyone to come out and try to persuade me back in. It was just that it all came over me all of a sudden, that was all, and I was leaning my head on the steering wheel when my phone rang. I let it ring for a bit, but at last I gave in. I expected it to be Heidi but it was Gavin. 'I'm sorry,' he said. I could imagine Heidi sitting there looking at him, glaring with an expression that meant: I'm really angry and if that doesn't work I don't mind crying for the rest of the day.

'I'm sorry,' he said again. 'Come back, why don't you. The kids want you to. Here.'

Now it was Jarvis on the line. 'Come back?' he said, somewhat uncertainly. 'Auntie Pam? Go on, please.' He was a nice kid and I could see him too, looking at his mum and at Gavin to be sure he was saying the right things.

It wasn't really me they wanted at all, I knew that. It was the Christmas dinner. Someone to cook the dinner was what they needed or rather – since they knew perfectly well that I was no cook – someone to blame when it all went wrong. That turkey in the oven, which I had collected and taken there the day before, meant a lot to them. Not that it was me who had ordered and paid for it; that had been – someone else. The turkey, and its sausages and stuffing and gravy and roast potatoes, all went to attest that Christmas would still be Christmas, just the same as ever, as Christmas had been ever since Jojo was a baby. It might be happening in Heidi's house instead of – somewhere else, but that was all right just so long as they could look around and know, or pretend, that all was right with their world. After all Christmas was variable. There was always something different – a new child, a different partner, occasionally one or another of our relatives doing us the honour of a visit. We had taken them in our stride. We could adapt to things like *that*. Like *this*, maybe not so easily.

I sighed really loudly to show them all that I was doing them a big favour – which I was, I absolutely was. 'All right,' I said. And I got out of the car and went back into the house, back to what I knew would be the worst Christmas I ever had, or will ever have, even though Christmas had always been for me, since Heidi was a child, a day of pretending. I could do that. I had pretended for more than thirty years that I didn't hate it; I had smiled and been helpful, and put myself last behind Heidi, and then her children, for whom, apparently, the whole weary frolic was invented. This year it would be harder, I expected, but all I had to do was bash about in the kitchen and present some kind of dinner, which would fall well short of its usual standard. Just as well. They would never forgive me if I managed to do it as well as – someone else.

And then I could make my escape when the two littlies went to bed, before Gavin and Heidi got down to some more rigorous drinking. I could leave before I could get into an argument with Gavin about the advisability of allowing Jojo a 'little sip' of Drambuie. Before Heidi started crying again, before I had to see Jarvis – who was sometimes the most grown-up person in that house – trying not to cry himself. Before they started feeding their misery and working themselves up to a satisfying hysteria, and trying to get me to do it too. Before they started accusing me of lacking proper feelings, I could drive home, or walk if necessary, or even ring for a taxi, I could be home by eight o'clock.

That was just about how it worked out. We got through the morning. The baby was put down for a sleep and we tackled the dinner. The turkey was dry and the roast potatoes undercooked and the gravy a bit on the watery side of perfection. The sprouts were nicely cooked – not too soft, but only Gavin and I would even attempt to eat them. No one was even mildly interested in food it seemed, let alone really hungry. There were crackers with jokes that only the grown-ups and Jarvis could either read or understand. Only Gavin and Jojo wanted Christmas pudding. There was a lot of everything left and I had a sick feeling that most of it would be thrown away –

someone would have been furious at that but I just felt sad and helpless.

Then we went back to the telly and what was left of the chocolate. Gavin, I was finding, as well as being boorish, was creepy in his insistence at making Heidi cry. It seemed Heidi had known him somehow for a while, but he had only recently become a live-in boyfriend. Partner, whatever you're supposed to call it. He seemed to me like some sort of hearse-chaser, never missing an opportunity to remind her – and the children and me – of what we in any case couldn't help thinking about. In his imagination he was Director of Mourning and I had to be present as he fed the children on chocolate and made them cry by telling them their nannan – he just couldn't grasp she was Granma – would have wanted them to be happy. So the mood was fragile, as Cassie and Jarvis and Heidi – and I – were dragged through incompatible emotions. Jojo looked at me occasionally, furtively, as if I was an interloper, or a ghost. Which I was I suppose. Jarvis looked anxious too, any time I said something remotely un-festive. Cassie called me Granma without realising her mistake and Gavin pointed out to her, in his most poisonous understanding voice, that I wasn't her nannan. Even the baby, who was too young to understand what sort of day it was, became more and more fractious and Gavin solved it by giving him more and more chocolate buttons. Heidi protested but only a little and he poured her more Prosecco and apologised for forgetting that she was grieving too.

By half past five I felt that I would not be missed if I went home. I fetched my bag from Cassie's room, put my coat on and stood in the doorway of the front room. 'I'll be off now,' I said. 'Thank you for –' I did not know what to say I was thanking them for. Heidi seemed to pull herself together enough to see me to the door when I left and touch me on the shoulder – she knew how I felt about the hugging that seemed to have become fashionable – and say thank you to me.

'We wouldn't have got through it without you,' she said. 'Are you doing anything for New Year?'

'No,' I said. I had no wish to join them for any more festivity. 'I'll just stay quietly at home.'

'I wonder then,' she said, 'I wonder could you have Jojo over to stay with you. Gavin wants us to invite his people round.'

'Maybe,' I said, but I knew that there was no maybe about it. I could see how things were going to pan out for the foreseeable future and I could not see that there was any way to stop it, or not any way that – someone – would approve of.

I expected to feel relieved to be out of here, and I did I suppose, but even before I'd turned the car for home the awful desolation and loneliness came over me and I had to stop driving and rest my head on the steering wheel once again.

It is not an experience we have ever contemplated repeating. These days Christmas still happens in their house, not mine. I am the old relative who has to be invited to dinner. I go, out of duty, Adam cooks, and I am always satisfied that I did go, and equally satisfied that I don't have to stay beyond what is polite. They must feel the same. They know what I'm like; reclusive, boring, critical, curmudgeonly. I am one of the burdens Heidi still has to bear.

On New Year's Eve – the last day of 2006 – it was Jarvis who walked over with his brother to my house, and they brought the damn dog as well.

'Mum said you'd be all right about it,' he said. 'It's just – Gavin's mum and dad are coming, and his auntie, and they say Gavin's mum's allergic you know, and we'd have to shut him in the kitchen, the dog I mean, and you know how he carries on, and then we'd have the neighbours complaining.'

'That's what they said?'

'Is it all right?' Jarv's face was pale, as it is always, and especially when he's worried. 'And he's company for Jojo isn't he. They love each other, dog and Jojo.' It sounded like something Gavin would say.

I could have refused. I had had to do quite a bit of clearing of my spare room so that Jojo could sleep in it. I'd already got the cat to look after. (Someone's cat. It turned up one day, wandering though my garden as if nothing had happened.) I'd already agreed to have Jojo. (Stupid name, always was even for a little kid, and now he's sixteen – but there's nothing I can do about it.) I could have sent Jarvis away with the dog and some well-chosen words. They were taking advantage of me – I knew it and they knew it – and ordinarily I would not have let them. But the times were not ordinary; the world was not as it had been. I shrugged, and made some sort of assenting noise because no one ever – I never – wanted to upset Jarvis; it wasn't his fault after all.

The dog – Vinny the dog – was one of our problems. After we went to the house – someone's bungalow, the day after it happened – and found the poor thing who'd been forgotten in all the disruption, howling and beside himself, well first of all, I took him home. He seemed to know what had happened. He carried on howling. He cried all night, and I felt like strangling him. Why should he be able to cry, and carry on so, when I was expected to maintain some sort of decorum? Next day I took him to Heidi's house, but he was no better there, and of course Heidi was no better than I was. It was upsetting for the children too, so she said, but they pleaded to keep him and she gave in to them, circumstances being what they were.

Daft name for a dog, Vinny, we all agreed; he was called after one of our brothers, who had died a good number of years ago. Similarly the cat was called Violet, after our aunt. Someone had the idea that animals deserved proper names, not infantile ones, or jokey ones, or recognised dog ones, but proper human names. She said it made them feel part of the family. She said it with a straight face and I never knew if she was joking. Probably she was.

'I wish I could stay,' said Jarvis. Jojo was already sitting in front of the TV. Special needs or not, he could handle a remote control.

'You can if you like,' I said.

'I can't,' he said. 'Mum needs me.'

Yes, I thought, you'll be upstairs keeping the little ones quiet while Gavin gets your mum drunk.

'Is his mum really allergic?'

'My mum says she's not. She says she only thinks she's most important person on the planet. I heard her say it to Gavin.'

I was pleased. They were beginning to argue, it would not be long before Gavin was down the road like all the others.

'Want to stay for a hot chocolate?'

'Better not,' he said.

Of all Heidi's children, Jarvis was the one I was most fond of and I was sad to see him slouch off down the road, hood up and hands in pockets. The dog was no substitute, though perhaps it helped to keep Jojo distracted from the discomfort of being with me. He knew me, he'd been to my house plenty of times, but it was clear that I, during those awful days, weeks and months, unsettled him. I knew why, I understood, but he didn't. I saw him looking at me, considering my voice, trying to make it make sense. He never confused us before, one with the other – but I suppose because he was still expecting her – someone – to come back he was constantly looking at me to make sure. Am I her, or still only me? And each time I disappointed. Each time I failed to be her.

We took the dog together for its evening walk round the block, avoiding the road where it used to live and we spent a peaceful evening in front of the TV, Jojo sitting with the dog – it was only a little thing, yappy, fluffy – on his lap, stroking it, and playing with its ears and talking to it in his own rudimentary way. Unintelligible muttering. I understood it was a comfort to him. I did *not* wish that *I* could take comfort from a dumb animal; I would have despised myself if I did, but for Jojo, simple, odd as he is, well, I was glad for him. If it slept on his bed – what do I mean, If? Of course it did – then that was a price worth paying for a quiet night and Heidi never needed to find out.

Jojo – real name Jordan - had had a difficult birth and that was why he was as he was. Is as he is. He doesn't have anything with a name, he doesn't have a syndrome or a recognised condition, he just has Learning Difficulties. Language Difficulties. The part of his brain that recognises language was damaged somehow. He's not deaf, he can even copy sounds, but it seems that he can't grasp the meaning of strings of words. Single words, not so bad – bed, yes, no, dinner, that sort of thing. But a sentence is too much, rather as it would be for me if a French person addressed me with a whole sentence. *Gauche. Droit. Merci.* I can manage them, but not a string of words one after the other with nothing to tell you where one ends and the next one starts. When you think of it, it's a wonder that most people *do* manage to understand, and poor old Jojo missed out on learning the trick of it. So when he's worried about something firstly it's impossible to know exactly what the problem is, and secondly difficult to reassure him. Heidi, naturally, is the best at it, and he will let her – and sometimes Jarvis but no one else – stroke and pat him. He likes food, except green vegetables; and television, and going in cars; is alarmed by motorbikes and by people in helmets of any kind, and by ambulances and fire engines; will sometimes visibly enjoy music, and will play the same album, or the same song even, time after time and then suddenly tire of it and switch to another one. To protect the rest of the world from the torment of this Heidi has made sure he has headphones.

He was a slight boy then, and pale, like Jarvis, with light brown floppy hair and a bit of a nervous tic. To myself I named his condition Living Difficulties. Because there was no way he would ever be able to survive on his own.

Once Christmas was over, and New Year, my life, like everyone else's, was supposed to return to normality. In previous years that is what must have happened – take down the decorations (not that I ever put any up), finish up the unloved chocolates at the bottom of the tin, write your thank you notes if you are that way inclined, abandon your resolutions, go back to work, begin anew. Well, that – beginning anew – that was going to have to happen, but it would not be normal. It would never go back to normal, not even to some new sort of normal. Rather like the days we are now in, perhaps.

It was all over – the news, the inquest, the funeral, the telling people, the changes, they had all been done. Christmas had come and gone, a New Year – 2007 – had begun, there was nothing for it *but* to begin anew. There was nearly a week before school started again and then there would be nothing for it but to go back there. I'd missed the end of term, naturally, but I couldn't any longer justify staying away. Maybe my GP would have signed me off again, but sooner or later it had to happen, I had to go back and face it. My days and evenings would be occupied by preparation work and the job of getting back in control of the loose threads I had left so suddenly, but there was spare, empty time too. Nothing to fill it.

I went for walks sometimes, just around the suburban streets, passing without seeing the sad dripping gardens and somehow always ending up outside her house, her bungalow, standing in the afternoon dusk, looking at the unlighted windows.

Often, in the evenings, my oldest sister Maureen would phone me. It was good of her, I knew, especially as she had her own domestic troubles – it was good of her and I hated it. She tried to be helpful – keep busy, she said, make sure you eat properly, get some fresh air. As if I needed or wanted her advice, as if I was about to follow any bit of it.

'I'm sure you've got some good friends around you,' she said. I did not reply and after she'd rung off I drank whisky and felt very sorry for myself. I didn't have friends. I had colleagues, many of whom I had known for quarter of a century; I had acquaintances and neighbours because I had lived in my house for more than twenty years. And I had a part-share, a very small part-share in *her* friends, in that I might be invited to go to the cinema with a group of them, or to the theatre if someone couldn't, at the last minute, use their ticket. I might be invited to a party, though I rarely accepted, and I might be included in a coffee in town if we happened to encounter one of *her* friends while we were doing some shopping. *Her* shopping, rarely mine.

This was how it had always been – I knew people but I didn't have friends. I couldn't think of a single person who I could call on for comfort or companionship or sympathy, I just couldn't. I had my colleagues, who remained nothing more than colleagues and I had family – my brothers and sisters who were well-meaning but distant in more ways than one, and Heidi who was nearby but who didn't like me any more than I liked her. This was how it was bound to stay.

On Sunday, the day before school started again, the weather was forecast to be good and I decided I would go out for a walk with the Ramblers; I'm not a constant presence on their walks but sometimes it's nice to walk with people instead of on my own. So they say. I drove out to Fox House to meet in the car park. I hoped nothing would be said but of course, there are always people who know your business, and people who would like to know your business, and so when someone said, 'I'm sorry for your trouble,'(which seemed to be what you had to say nowadays) someone else said, 'What? Has something happened?'

'My sister died,' I said.

'Oh I'm sorry,' she said, conforming to my recently devised Scale of Expressed Sorrow, in which the least compassion is expressed for the death of a sibling, a little more for an aged parent, still more for a spouse, with real shock and pity presumably kept for occasions when a child or grandchild has met an untimely end.

Another woman – so muffled in scarf and hat that I wasn't sure if I knew her or not, said, 'Was it expected?'

'No,' I said.

'Always worse,' she said, 'when it's a shock.'

'No doubt,' I said.

'You don't want to talk about it?' she said with a hopeful lift to her voice, whether hoping I did or didn't I couldn't tell.

'No,' I said.

Then one of the men changed the subject. 'Now, you're in the Local History Group aren't you?' he said.

'I've been a couple of times,' I said. 'But it's not really for me.' (They were a funny lot, I thought, some of them quite scholarly and very pedantic, and some rather woolly and inclined to get excited only when they found a gravestone with a name on it that might have been some great-great aunt or other of their cousin in Australia. Things like that. So after going to one or two meetings – well it was only the second time I went – I lost patience with some long-winded man who was nit-picking about the Chartists and never went again.)

'There are some good people there,' he said, 'but some of them are a bit inclined to get bogged down in detail, it's true.'

I said nothing. I'd known this man, Terry, on and off for years, and by and large I liked him so I didn't want to be too rude. I had worked with him some years ago, before he left for a more senior post in another school, from which he had now retired. I believed he had even been at the funeral, but as he didn't mention it, neither did I.

'I'll tell you why I'm asking,' he said. 'We're looking for someone – someone who knows what they're doing both in terms of the history and in terms of walking – we're on the lookout for someone who could put together a history walk booklet that follows the path of the Sheffield Flood.'

'Haven't you got someone who does that sort of thing?' I said to him.

'Lionel's our flood expert,' he said, 'but he's not very mobile these days.'

'He's not that much of an expert,' I said.

'Maybe not,' said Terry. 'Now, I know you've got other things taking up your time –'

I may have looked at him quite sharply at that point; I was not in need of any more sympathy, thank you all the same.

'– what I mean to say is,' he said, 'there's no hurry for this. We'd much prefer it to be good, rather than quick. If it works out well we can print a good few copies and put them in the libraries, and the Tourist Information. But there's no deadline – at least not until twenty-fourteen. Anniversary you know.'

'Thinking ahead then,' I said.

'In your own time,' he said.

I was grateful to Terry for not saying the words, 'to take your mind off your troubles' or 'to keep your spirits up.' Nothing, I was very aware, would take my mind off what had happened, and my spirits as they were – low – were perfectly congruent with the state of affairs.

You might think anyway – I would not blame you – that a person's spirits might not be lifted by contemplating a major incident that claimed the lives of upwards of two hundred and forty people, including children, and you would be right, but I didn't want my spirits lifted. It wouldn't feel proper; I wouldn't be me.

'I'll think about it,' I said.

Now of course, these days, the Ramblers are not allowed to meet. Even if they walked the prescribed two metres from each other, and never offered to share a packet of crisps, they would not be allowed. Too many people, too many germs being propelled into the air, contagion, infection, plague – these are our preoccupations these days. It was reported that Derbyshire police used drones to spot gatherings of people and then made them get back in their cars and go home. As if there wasn't enough room in Derbyshire. Well, they say, now you can exercise at home, there's virtual yoga and Pilates, online is crammed with exercise videos and virtual workouts so who needs the countryside and greenery and real fresh air.

They – the radio, the papers – are predicting what they call lockdown, as has happened in other countries. My brother Alan, when he phones me says he is stockpiling groceries and cleaning equipment; he has told his sons, all four of them, to do the same. Myself, I can't believe it will come to that sort of crisis. No one *I* know has got it, or had it, or even knows anyone who has it. It's only flu. Isn't it?

One of the hard parts, I was finding, back then, was saying her name. My brain had been stopping short of it for weeks; it was almost as if I had forgotten it, I had so successfully suppressed it. At first I could say it. Her name. I had to tell people. I had to tell Heidi, first of all, then my remaining sisters and brothers. I had to tell them at school, I had to let her friends know. I had to register the death, I had to help arrange her funeral, before that I had to sit through the inquest. I had to say it and I said it. I have no memory of how it felt. To say it. Now, I can't even think it. My brain veers away from it, the words don't even come into my mind, the words: her, my sister, my twin sister, her name. She, *she,* comes into my mind a million times a day, she never leaves it, but the words – the words will not be thought, let alone said.

We had not always worked in the same school. I had been there ever since I qualified, longer than anyone else except Frank Midgeley, but *she* had done the rounds of schools, staying in each one for a year or two, maybe four or five years, then saying she was bored, or didn't like some colleague or other, fancied a change, and moved on. Eventually – this was about three years before – she joined our establishment. At first it was a bit of a novelty and then it stopped feeling anything but normal. Everyone got used to it. I was History, she was Food Technology. Everyone was fine with it, it was taken for granted. Miss Dearly History, Miss Dearly Cooking. What was difficult about that?

Not that We saw each other very much at work. Though We lived close to each other We mostly made our separate ways into school; she liked to get there early to set up her room for the day, and to leave as early so she could get home to take the dog out, and then go and help Heidi with the children. I tended to stay later after school; there were meetings that involved me, there was department business, and I had nothing special to get home for. We were on different year teams, different duty teams, so We met rarely inside school, and in fact though I was full-time, she only worked four days a week, so there could be one whole day in a week where I didn't see her at all. I thought I would not miss her presence at school except as a general concept of missing her. That was my belief.

There in the staff room, in front of the array of pigeonholes – hers and mine both stuffed with paper – why, when we all have email? – there it was, her name, in front of me, assaulting my eyes. I pulled out the stack of papers – Christmas cards, reminders, form lists, incident reports, a questionnaire – and put them all, hers and mine, without looking at them at all – in the bin. I thought I heard a small gasp of shock from someone behind me but I took no notice and whoever it was said nothing.

My form – 11PD – had obviously been briefed. Not that they would need it, having known me as they had for more than four years already. They were quieter than usual, guarded, tentative. When a couple of the boys came into the room loudly they were hissed at to watch themselves and they hushed up immediately. I was touched by their concern. I was proud of their maturity and the evidence that they knew how I prefer to be dealt with. I could imagine – if it had been the other way round and it was me that had died – how *her* girls would be even now offering hugs and little gifts of chocolate to my sister and the boys would be shuffling and behaving especially well, but my lot knew to leave me alone and just behave themselves.

I got through the week. This is what happens, you get through. You might not remember much about what you did and what you said; you might not notice the weather, or whether someone is speaking to you or not; you might find that you haven't drunk your coffee and it is sitting cold on the staff room table. But you still breathe, you still manage to eat and drink after a fashion, you remember to go to the toilet. You walk or drive home without getting lost, you feed the cat – *her* cat that is, which I seemed to have inherited permanently and no, I did not find it a comfort. It was a nuisance.

I got through the week. There were decisions to be made about exam entries. I took all the Year Eleven work home and sorted through it, judging their progress and their predicted grades. The exercise books from my other classes were in various kinds of chaos, depending who had been looking after them during my absence. I got them back into some sort of order and marked all their work, so that they would know I was on top of things.

Heidi phoned. 'When should we start on the bungalow?' she said. 'This weekend?'

Our houses – not mine and Heidi's, mine and *hers* – were quite close to each other. From my back bedroom window I could see the roof of her bungalow; from her front garden she could look up and see the lime trees at the bottom of my garden. Most evenings I could look out of my front window at around half-past nine and she would be going past, taking the dog for his last walk of the day. If I wanted to speak to her I would tap on the window and she would come in; if she wanted to speak to me she would come in through the back door without having to knock. Probably four or five evenings every week We met, sometimes just standing in my hallway, bringing back something she'd borrowed, or maybe she would be asking, Had I heard from Alan or another one of our siblings, or I would want to know did she have any use for my surplus blackcurrants? Other times she would come properly into the house and We would have tea and cake and spend the evening talking together.

Or maybe at a weekend she might phone me and ask if I had time to go round and give her a hand with something – moving a sofa, or holding the ladder while she pruned her clematis. I always told her she pruned that clematis too much and that was why it never flowered to any extent but she was a tidier gardener than I am and she liked to keep her plants under control. She was tidier in every way actually. Often at my house she would put her tea cup down, pushing aside a pile of stuff to make space for it, and tell me, quite mildly, that I was worse than Heidi for living in chaos and that I didn't have the excuse that Heidi had. And I would tell her that I knew where everything was and could put my hand instantly on whatever I wanted – which however, was not really true.

I did understand that Heidi wanted to sell the bungalow. I understood that she needed the money, though I hoped she would keep it out of the hands of the likes of Gavin. I did not begrudge her the money, though I was not convinced she would use it wisely. I had already spent time there – finding documents, address book, bank details, school keys, all that sort of thing. I had taken the perishable food too, and turned off the fridge, and turned down the central heating to frost protection only. I had also taken some of her stuff. I don't know why I did that; it was a sort of feeling of No-one-else-can-have-that as I stumbled around the rooms that had been her home and did not want to be there and could not make myself close the door and be outside of it. I took the book she seemed to have been reading – it was a Jack Reacher novel and I knew I would never read it myself, but it was there on her coffee table, open, face down, next to the TV remote and her old reading glasses. I took things I wanted to keep out of Heidi's hands – things relating to our parents, and our nan, certificates, letters, things like that, and some ornaments from our Auntie Vi's house which I had always hated, but not hated enough to let Heidi sell them on e-bay. I took her umbrella, though it wasn't raining, just because I saw it there in the hall, and from the bedroom I took a cardigan that was draped over the back of a chair and her dressing gown that was lying across her bed.

There was much more work to be done and though I did not want to go back in there it was also true that there were more things I would like to have and I couldn't be sure that Heidi would not throw them out, or take them for herself. I knew as well that there was the possibility of Heidi and I disagreeing and I wanted to put it off as long as I could.

'What about the children?' I said. 'It won't be easy with them around.'

'Jarvis can look after them,' she said.

'What about Jojo?'

'He could help us.'

'Don't be ridiculous,' I said. 'Jojo's not capable of being any help and he'll go to pieces if he gets inside her place, you know that. Can't Gavin look after him?'

'He's not really that good,' she said – whether talking about Jojo or Gavin I wasn't sure. 'Maybe Jarv could keep an eye on him as well.'

'You ask too much of that boy,' I said. 'Anyway, I'm busy this weekend. I need a bit more notice than two days you know.'

And no, I didn't feel mean. I was not going to settle into someone else's role. Heidi had to learn to sort her life out for herself.

I lied when I said I was busy. I was making up small jobs for myself, tidying drawers, throwing away minor items. I sorted – this is how desperate I was – I sorted out all the rusty paper clips and threw them away. I sewed on a couple of buttons and tidied the sewing box. After I put the lid back on and put it in its usual place on the floor, I went back to it and searched for any rusty pins that I could throw away. The big pile of cards, however, Christmas cards and sympathy cards, all mixed in together, stayed unsorted. I took them off the sideboard, mostly still in envelopes, and put them into a Tesco bag and pushed it to the back of the cupboard in the hall.

I looked at the pile of things on my spare room bed, things that did not and never had belonged there, that needed seeing to and sorting and putting away, things that needed to be kept from Heidi's eyes. I picked up a cardigan, a photograph album, a cardboard file of papers, a jewellery box, and put each one down again without looking at it.

I walked round the garden, though it was not possible to do any gardening as yet. It had rained, and snowed, and rained again, and the ground was soaked, so walking on it, even to tidy up, wasn't advisable. The alchemilla leaves were brown and soggy, everything else was sticks, except the little weeds that were coming up everywhere. Even weeds might be seen, on a good day, as a sign of recovery, and spring, and regeneration, but I could only think what a nuisance they were going to be. It's true that there were snowdrops pushing through and there were flower buds on the hellebores, but I could not feel cheered. However welcome, the first sight of snowdrops and hellebores are minor, funereal sorts of things – it's a quiet satisfaction you get from them, not a sudden onset of gaiety; and even satisfaction felt way beyond me.

I went inside and felt straightaway that I had to go out again. This was happening all the time, wanting to be in when I was out, and out when I was in. I got in my car and drove round to the next street – her street – and let myself into her garden. Hers was much tidier – she had taken out the annuals and cut all the rest down at the end of the summer, though I always told her not to – and I couldn't find much to do, except to sweep up a few leaves in the corners, and wonder what she was growing in her pots. I had never been one for a lot of pots but I was going to have hers. I carried them one by one to the car – her next door neighbour watched me out of the front window but I did not acknowledge her – and stacked them in the boot. Heidi wasn't going to get a single one, she would only neglect it, or break it. I left the three in the front garden – they were too heavy for me to move and besides I thought they softened the front garden and made the house look more lived-in. I didn't like to think of it empty.

And here I am, now, in these days, in her house, actually living in her house, and in spite of all the years I've been here, it still feels like her house. Not mine. I know how I came to be here, I can explain it but I still can't quite believe it. I liked *my* house. It suited me. It was shabby and untidy and neglected, and there was more stuff in it than there were cupboards to put stuff into, but I didn't care and saw no reason to change it. Not, I insist, that I was ever one of those deranged hoarders you sometimes see on TV if you don't turn it off quick enough – I just kept things I wanted to keep, and I wasn't all that good at being tidy. Now, most of my stuff has gone; this little toy house I'm in now just couldn't cope with it all. So I de-cluttered, as they insist on saying nowadays, and now I live in a manner that my sister, if she could see me, would have disapproved of a bit less.

It's not her house as she knew it. It looks different, it smells different, but still it's hers and it's certainly not mine. The furniture is mine – hers went to Heidi, or was sold; I wouldn't have wanted it anyway, our tastes being different from each other once we were no longer children. I took all her pictures down and gave them away to different people in the family – landscapes mostly, or vases of flowers. I never replaced them with anything. Her curtains are still up at the windows, though I never use the fancy tie-backs – they just hang there looking useless and I keep thinking I should take them away, except that they are things she made herself. I almost do it, and then I don't.

'I don't want a big house,' she said to me more than once. 'A small one is fine as long as you're organised. Just put things back where they belong when you've finished using them. Tidy things away. Every day, not once a week.'

She knew that even once a week would have been too much for me. Maybe in the summer holidays I would make an effort to sort things out a little, but then I would usually be working in the garden. Now, of course, confined as we are, would be the perfect time to sort out my belongings, except that I don't have most of them any more.

She would have been furious at being told to stay at home. She would have kicked against being told not to see her daughter, her grandchildren, her friends. She would have been looking for ways to go

26

out, to get round the regulations. 'You need to get out more.' – nobody ever said that to her.

And with Jarvis' baby due any day – imagine telling her that she couldn't go to see her great-grandchild, couldn't sweep into the hospital ward with flowers and baby clothes, couldn't take a million photos with her phone and send them to everyone she knew. Actually she died before she possessed a phone that could take photos but if she were still here she would have one, I know she would.

But everything has to shut down. After this weekend children will not return to school. There will be nowhere to go – can't get a cup of coffee, can't get your hair cut, can't go and see a film or a play or a concert or go to a gym or a swimming pool. Not that any of these prohibitions are going to spoil my life because I don't as a rule do any of them. Me, I sit and I remember, and I write down what I remember, and then I remember some more.

Brogging End to Upper Thornseats

CSE Local History
Dale Dyke Dam Disaster
Worksheet 1

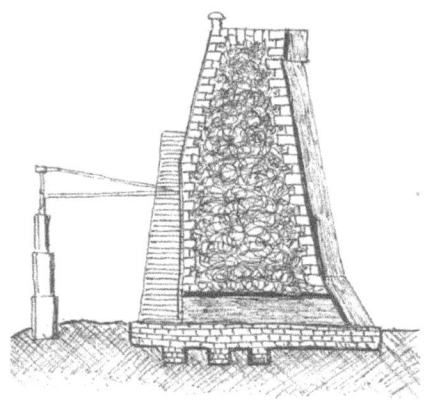

1. Copy and label the diagram of the dam.
2. Explain why dams were being built.

When I first came to Sheffield I had never heard of the Great Dale Dyke Dam Disaster. They don't make that much of it in Sheffield, never mind in far away places that have their own floods to care about. But I like to think, even now, that there's a generation of schoolchildren, all now thirty years older, more even, who did know about it, and maybe even told their own children, and dragged them protesting up the Loxley valley to see where it all began.

Sunday I decided it would be a good thing to go for a walk. Not so much *decided* as felt that I had to do something. I was too restless to stay indoors, I couldn't settle, I couldn't even sit. It was too late to join with the Ramblers, and anyway I hadn't enjoyed the last time I went with them so I thought I would go up to the reservoir and see if I really did feel up to starting on a project.

I parked my car and walked down the track to the reservoir. Not the downstream end where the dam was built, but the top end, where the water runs in from the Dale Dyke and from all the surrounding moors. January was halfway through and there was snow patched in crevices and along the north side of the drystone walls. There were snowdrops there too, growing wild, showing white at the tips, pushing through the leaf litter by the side of the path. As the track bent round there were some old farm buildings, empty now. I wondered if I should research who might have lived there a hundred and fifty years ago. What would they have thought of the hundreds of navvies who were changing their landscape and flooding their fields? But they were not part of the story; there was plenty of material without them.

The dam is of course at the other end, and I had never walked along this path before. When I used to bring the school kids out here as part of their Local History course – in the days when there could *be* such a thing as a local history course – we only looked at the dramatic spot where the dam gave way and then got back in the minibus and went on down the valley. But the reservoir itself will need a paragraph and I can lift it from my old notes – that's one of the good things about history I used to think, school history at least – the notes didn't change with the fashion. But I was wrong, they do.

"The Sheffield Waterworks Company began construction on the dam in 1859. Its purpose was to provide water to power the mills and grinding wheels along the River Loxley and to supply water to the growing population of Sheffield."

When the water came into view it was the colour of dull metal. To me the reservoir looked full, as it should at that time of the year.

I met no one as I walked along the bridleway, looking down on the water. Walking by myself – well, it wasn't a new experience. I was not and am not a person who relies on company. But walking alone accentuated everything. I couldn't point anything out to a companion, I couldn't say, Look, is that a kestrel? I couldn't complain about the wind, or the mud, I didn't have someone else to notice the things I had missed seeing. I had only my own eyes, my own thoughts. That was why I walked with the Ramblers sometimes, because it's good for one, so it is said, to have some social interaction. At least, I thought, this is not a walk I ever did with –her – this is not going to bring out any half-forgotten remembrances.

I almost never walked with – her. I sometimes bullied her into doing a proper walk with me but really the most she ever wanted to do was to take her ridiculous dog round the block two or three times a day, so I had very few memories of her out in the wide outdoors. But I thought about her all the same.

It was a horrible path, muddy and slippery and sloping in ways that made it even more likely that a person could end up flat on their back in a slimy puddle. I had no idea why I was doing what I was doing. I had noticed nothing, I had gained nothing. I wanted to be at home; I wanted it with an ache that for a moment replaced the normal ache, and when I saw a footpath going off to the left I took it, and decided that this whole scheme was going nowhere. Who, anyway, would think that this end of the reservoir was part of the story? It had no history; it was irrelevant as well as uncomfortable and boring. I was giving up.

I walked back up a darkening road to where I had left the car. What daylight there had been had gone and I saw no one except two hikers in the distance. I drove back home to Grenoside through Bradfield and Oughtibridge and resisted the pull in me to drive past the bungalow. It never did any good. It would have been better, I knew, to get on and clear it, and sell it. It would be better to close that door and know that other people were going to be there, making their own life. What difference could it make anyway, to me? There was no comfort, there was no forgetting. Everything reminded me. I could have shut myself up in a cupboard with nothing to see or hear and something would still have come back to me, something to nag and prick and trouble me, something she said, or did, or had, or saw, or something she didn't see, or do. Et cetera.

Where We lived is on the northern edge of Sheffield, uphill, out of the valley. If I walked out of my house and away from the village – suburb really – I could walk across squelchy fields, or along the road past the crematorium entrance, and I would come to open country where the ground falls away and you can look over the valley. I could see farms and stables and then, looking towards the city, landmarks – the Arts Tower at the university, the television mast at Crosspool. Look the other way and there were the hills of Derbyshire, and between them the valleys that hold the reservoirs that hold the water we use thoughtlessly and easily. Down there, straight down, flows the River Don.

We, neither of us, had ever been comfortable too near water. The seaside wouldn't do for us at all. Nor any flat country, which people think is strange considering that We spent our lives until We came here to college, in Essex, that flattest of counties. Our brothers and sisters were still there, most of them, but We got away. We came north together, on a coach from Victoria up the M1, on our way to be interviewed at the old teacher training college and We had never seen before in all our lives what We saw beside the road – rocks, big chunks of stone, bare and sticking out of the ground. The road through

Derbyshire had been cut through rock, visible, brown rock, shiny in places. If you dug down east of London all you would find was clay, and the water table. We were entranced, fascinated and that was probably one of the reasons that Sheffield swung it for us instead of Bishop's Stortford or Trent Park.

When I was home I made myself a cup of tea and some toast, and fed the cat. I searched out my boxes of schoolwork, and there they were at the bottom of the first box – the whole package of Local History CSE work, not used or looked at since the revolution of the National Curriculum and the blending of CSE and GCE. Something like 1985 I was thinking. I had material on Bishop's House and Manor Castle, and slum clearance, on steel production and the gang wars, some copies of the words of a song called The Grinders' Hardships, worksheets and photographs and instructions for coursework projects. I could see them, the kids, piling out of the minibus, grabbing their clipboards and pens, shoving and jostling and talking and – occasionally – *looking* at what we were there to see, and listening and learning. Remembering? Who knows? I extracted the pages with anything I thought might be relevant – though it turned out that many of the items were missing – and put them on my dining table (which I never use for dining) along with the local history books and pamphlets I've collected over the years and kept. As if it was ever going to come back on the school curriculum.

All the work I had done on local, interesting, relevant, accessible events, things I could take the minibus full of fifteen year olds to see, the big houses where the Sheffield businessmen and steelmakers lived, the cottages where still you could see the workshops in the backs where the little mesters finished off the goods, the canal, the lost railway village of Parkwood Springs, the first ever football club, the places where the gangs ran their illegal gambling operations. My kids may never have got good grades for the subject, but they left school knowing something of where they came from, having some connection with the past of the place where they lived.

I look back at the inventive and committed person I must have been then. Did I really do all that? What happened?

Well, thirty-odd years happened. History happened. ('Oh Miss,' moaned one of my twelve year olds, 'Miss I hate history. It goes on for *ever.*' Hm.)

It seemed as if I had made the decision to do it. To compose a leaflet for Terry and his history group. Maybe not quite a decision, not exactly a commitment, not a definite but a perhaps. Maybe.

So, start at the bottom end of the Dale Dyke reservoir, I decided. Bradfield, Loxley, Hillsborough, Neepsend, Kelham Island, The Wicker. You'd need to be fit to do it down and back in one go but that's OK. And by definition there's not a lot to see. Most of what got washed away has stayed washed away, what was rebuilt is different from what was there then. *Then* there were people sleeping four to a bed, sleeping in cellars, on top of boxes, *in* boxes, households full of children, lodgers, dogs, servants; relatives and friends staying overnight because there was no transport to go home. 'You kids,' I used to tell them,' you don't know you're born.'

Late in the evening – just as I was packing my bag for work the next day – I had a phone call from my oldest brother, Eddie. It was becoming very obvious to me that my siblings – my remaining siblings, three brothers and two sisters – had set up a rota. Every day or two, one or other of them would call me. They were all a long way away, and it was nice of them, I was supposed to think, to remember that I was on my own now. It was good of them to try to help me through the days. I was profoundly untouched by it all though, only irritated when it was Alan's turn, because he tended to get emotional. But this evening it was Eddie.

Eddie was already sixteen when We were born, and he went into the army for his National Service before We were able to differentiate him from Jimmy, his twin. So, he asked how I was and I didn't answer directly, just said I'd been back at work and it was fine, and he asked after Heidi and the children and I said they were OK, and pretty quickly he handed me over to his wife, Olive, and she asked the same things and I gave the same answers.

'At least,' she said, 'there's no husband for us to worry about.'

'What's that supposed to mean?' I said. I could have stopped myself but in fact I didn't try to. I had been feeling, earlier in the evening almost what might pass for normal, but the feeling had gone.

'Oh now Pam,' she said. 'I don't mean to say we don't worry about *you*. You know we do. If there's anything –' and then I took pity on her, or maybe on myself and said I was going now to have a bath, and thank you for calling. Et cetera.

I didn't have a bath. I had a glass of whisky and watched whatever appeared on the TV when I switched it on, and later, well past my proper bedtime, I went and got into bed, without cleaning my teeth. This was not like me.

I was putting in a lot of hours of school work, trying to get kids to revision sessions and chivvying them about coursework. My own form group were pretty good but there were still one or two who hadn't applied to college or sixth form – one of them, Daisy, a bright girl who seemed to be heading on a self-destructive path, was worrying me. I ought to set up a meeting with her mother. Also meetings with the parents of both Kane and Josh – though I doubted whether I could get their parents to attend – after so many meetings probably from Infants' School onward, they must have been looking forward as much as I was to the day they could be shot of school and all its unreasonable demands.

Mondays were when we had our weekly staff meeting after school, which was brutal, but got it out of the way for the week.

It was dark when I got home and by my headlights I could see a person sitting on my garden wall. I pulled off the road and saw, as I got out of the car, that it was Jarvis.

'All right?' he said. There was a biting wind and it was threatening to snow; he was hunched with cold and his voice was shaky.

'Come in and get warm,' I said.

Once he'd sat in the kitchen for a bit, in the warmth, and had a mug of hot chocolate and a few biscuits, I thought it was time to ask what he was doing, so uncharacteristically, outside my house in the dark.

It took a while to get anything out of him. He was pale – he's always pale these days – and his mouth was quivery, and I guessed he had had a row with his mum.

'Not Mum,' he said.

'Gavin then?'

He nodded.

'Want to tell me?'

He started to cry then, though he tried hard not to. I had never understood this until recently, that you can want all you like *not* to cry, but there are times when it will happen, like it or not, and trying to stop it happening only makes your sobs louder and snottier and go on for longer. 'Don't cry' is probably the world's least helpful phrase one person can say to another. I passed him a roll of kitchen towel and waited until he could speak.

'Dog,' he said at last. 'Vinny.'

'What happened?' I said, surmising that he had perhaps run out into the road in front of a car, and feeling slightly queasy at the thought.

'Gavin.'

'What has Gavin done?'

Jarvis wiped his hand across his nose and looked down at his knees. 'Had him put down,' he muttered, and sniffed wetly.

That *did* upset me. 'What did your mum say?'

'She screamed at him. She told him to get out.'

'So she didn't know about it?'

'No. He just went and did it. He didn't say nothing, not to Mum or anybody. Then he came home and said, and it was like he wanted us to be glad.'

I could imagine it. I could imagine too that Heidi had said things that allowed Gavin to think he was doing what she wanted – a sort of Thomas a Becket moment, a 'who will rid me of this troublesome dog' moment. Because Vinny had not forgotten his mistress and although he would be quiet if Jojo or Jarvis were stroking him, he still howled most nights, and clawed at the doors and windows as if he would run away if he got the chance. Heidi had enough to take care of, without a bereaved and neurotic lap dog and I had some sympathy with her. I hoped though, that there really was no afterlife, because – someone – would be upset if she was looking down and knew about Vinny. No, not just upset – she'd be furious.

He took Vinny to a vet, I know that much because later he passed the bill to me to be settled out of my sister's money (of which there was, of course, none). So at least he didn't drown him, or go through some gruesome process in the back garden.

'I didn't know you were so fond of it,' I said.

He looked at me as if I had said something stupid. 'It was *her* dog,' he said.

Oh the damage, the concentric rings of damage after a death. It's a wonder the human race survives.

'Maybe he thought he was being helpful,' I said. This was insincere of me and Jarvis knew it.

'*You* don't like Gavin do you,' he said.

'No I don't. Do you?'

'He can be a bit horrible,' he said, carefully.

'He is in fact,' I said, 'a totally unpleasant human being, the worst yet.'

Jarvis did not say he agreed but then possibly his life experience might have taught him that there were worse men in the world. Which there are, though I hoped he hadn't met them.

I made him more hot chocolate and gave him unopposed access to the biscuit tin. We sat at the table and crumbled our Hobnobs in silence.

'Can I stay here?' he said.

I thought about my very untidy spare bedroom and all the boxes and papers and bags I would have to move for him to sleep there, and I said, 'I suppose so. I'd have to do a bit of clearing up.'

'I'll help you,' he said. He really was not like a normal teenager.

'Go and ring your mum,' I said. 'Tell her I'll drop you off at school tomorrow.'

But as it turned out I had no need to move as much as a single box or pair of curtains off the bed. Jarvis handed the phone to me without speaking.

'Heidi?' I said. 'Problem?'

'Send him home,' she said. 'He shouldn't be at yours anyway, I need him here, he knows that.'

'He's very upset,' I said. 'He needs a bit of space.'

'We're all upset,' she said. 'What sort of state do you think Jojo's in? How do you think I feel? I want him home.'

'Let me just give him his tea,' I said. It was not like me to try to be diplomatic.

'I've told you what I want,' she said. 'You're being as bad as my mother. He doesn't need spoiling you know. Will you bring him home, or do I have to come and get him?'

Jarvis was hearing all this and he whispered to me, 'Is Gavin there? Ask her, is Gavin there. I'm not going if he's there.'

'Why don't you send Gavin to come and pick him up,' I said, cunningly.

'He's not here,' she said.

'All right,' said Jarvis. 'I'll go.'

He stroked the cat for longer than I thought was possible before we got into the car, and I drove him home to Chapeltown.

'Are you coming in?' he said hopefully when I stopped the car.

'Sorry Jarv,' I lied. 'I've got a lot on this evening. Good luck.'

As I drove away Heidi's car came too fast into their road and I could see it was Gavin driving it.

Though now Gavin is long gone. And his replacement, Adam, remarkably, is still around, still living with Heidi, apparently happily; and Heidi has had no more children which to my mind is a good thing.

She phones to tell me that Paige, Jarv's partner, has given birth to a little girl. She is to be called – poor child – Pollyanna, and of course no one can go and see her, but Heidi says why don't I call round this afternoon and she will show me the photos Jarv has sent.

Well, I think to myself, this might be the last time I get to see anyone for weeks, so I might as well go, even though I am the last person to say the right thing when looking at pictures of a baby. So I put on a more respectable pair of trousers and go round to the next street where Heidi lives – where *I* should still live – to be sociable.

Cassie opens the door to me. 'Did you hear?' she says.

'About the baby?'

'About the exams.'

'Yes I heard. No exams.'

She looks pretty gleeful about it. 'My mocks were OK,' she says. 'As long as I can go to six form college I don't care.'

Heidi comes down the stairs. 'Go in,' she says. 'You don't have to wait to be asked. Ros is already there anyway.'

I know why she's sending me in there instead of letting me into the back of the house – it's because I always make some comment on the state of the garden. I can't help it. That was *my* garden. I understood, at first, that Heidi had small children and letting them trash the flower beds and ride bikes on the grass paths was to be expected – but now, by now she could have done something about it. When I tell her though, things like she should prune the roses, I would show her how to do it, or Jarvis would, and she should pull out the weeds, or let me do it, she ignores me, just pretends she hasn't heard, changes the subject. Once or twice, when I've really got on her nerves, she's made a comment about how the house at least is clean and tidy, implying, justifiably, that when it was my house the garden was pretty near perfect and the house was a rubbish dump. So we keep up the pretence that we are on bad terms, not wishing to acknowledge the goodwill that exists. We are family after all.

Ros is Adam's mother, and quite why she's muscling in on an occasion which is nothing to do with her I don't know. She lives out at Hathersage and I've met her before only rarely, and never really taken to her, although I like Adam very much, especially when I compare him to some of his predecessors. His mother is a small, elegant, embittered woman who thinks that because she once trained in some para-medical skill – physiotherapy I think – that gives her the knowledge and the right to lecture people about their health and lifestyle, and advise them to do yoga, like she does. She is the sort of person who will ask a personal question, about what you eat, or how well you sleep, for example, misunderstand the answer you give and go on to educate you by telling you her way of doing it. She smiles at me, showing off her nice whitened teeth, only taking notice of me because Cassie and Jojo are taking no notice of her.

Jojo – although he answers to the name Jordan now, and about time too – is sitting with headphones on listening to what he is watching on TV; on the screen insects seem to be eating each other.

'Hi there Jordan,' I say, but he can't hear me on account of the headphones. Jayden is nowhere to be seen, which is pretty normal for a kid who's nearly fourteen and about to be plunged into social isolation.

'Hello Pamela,' says Ros. 'How does it feel to be a great-great-aunt?'

'Fine,' I say shortly, although actually, hearing that very aging term makes me feel not only old but quite disorientated. How did that happen?

'Is this your first great-great niece?' she says.

'I should say not,' I say, 'since I'm the youngest of eight children. I have a nephew who is the same age as I am.' A lie but only a small one.

'How does that work?' says Cassie. She is the only one of the children who takes the slightest interest in my – and her – extended family. Jarvis did, briefly, once, but now has more important things to concern him.

'Well,' says Ros chirpily, 'we're only as old as we feel aren't we.'

'Or look,' I say. She is very skinny, which makes her much more wrinkly than me, but she doesn't seem to be offended. Probably hasn't understood what I'm getting at.

'Dreadful times,' she says. 'They say it could go on for weeks.'

'Months,' I say.

'Oh no,' she says, as if she has a hotline to the Chief Medical Officer. 'I'm sure it's only a precaution. We'll be back to normal by Easter, surely.'

'We'll see,' I say, and luckily at that moment Heidi comes in with a tray of tea and cakes, Adam following.

We have to wait for the end of Jordan's programme before we can look at the baby photos because they are to be played through the TV somehow. Yes I know it's not exactly new technology but it's a process I have never had to bother with; I don't take photos anyway. Even when they show up on the screen there's not a lot to see – shot after shot of a squashed little red face wrapped in a blanket, Paige looking flushed and over-excited like a child. Then one of Jarvis, looking pale and shaken, holding the baby and looking as if he doesn't know what to do with his face. That's about it and we can get on with eating cake, and talking about the virus.

'There's that place,' says Cassie. 'We've been there, where they all died. They put their money in jars of vinegar.'

'What?' says Ros.

'I know what you mean,' I say. 'You're talking about Eyam, out in Derbyshire. Not far from where you live, Ros.'

'That's it,' says Cassie. 'They all got the Black Death and died.'

'Thanks for that,' says Heidi.

'I had a book about it,' says Cassie. 'You remember.'

'I remember,' I say. I remember buying it for her, typical history teacher's present. 'Berlie Doherty wrote it, *Children of Winter* it's called. It was about the plague, in the seventeenth century – not the Black Death, that was earlier.'

'Were they the same disease?' says Adam, and I have to admit that I don't know, but Heidi has it on her phone within seconds – 'Yes, same thing, bubonic plague, rats, fleas, bring out your dead. OK? Can we talk about something else now?'

But it seems that we can't.

That was Saturday; this is Sunday. Heidi phones me. Adam's mother has developed a dry cough.

'She says she hasn't got a temperature,' Heidi says, 'but we were all there with her – she's probably just being dramatic – but we should all be quarantined.'

'Nonsense,' I say, or something like it. 'I kept well away from her. She didn't breathe on me I can promise you.'

'Pam,' said Heidi – I can hear her being exasperated with me. 'You could have touched something she touched. Doorknobs. Tea cups. You have to stay in for a fortnight. You've got food in your freezer haven't you.'

It is funny, I think, that someone like Heidi who has always been a bit of a rebel, keen on having her own way, a never-mind-the-consequences sort of woman, has suddenly become not only an expert on this stupid new state of affairs, but absolutely signed up to all the restrictions and recommendations that she can find online and on the news.

It shouldn't bother me. I don't go out much anyway. I don't see people. But now that I'm officially not allowed to do the things I didn't do before, I want to do them. I feel cheated. I feel imposed upon. I feel grumpy.

My brother Alan has always been a great one for keeping in touch – which by the way is a strange term for a process that involved a complete lack of touch. After – someone – died he was on the phone almost every day. A lot of 'darlins', a lot of sighing.

'Halfway though January,' he said, as if I didn't know.

'Still raining,' I said.

'Seven weeks since,' he said.

I did not say anything.

'Now then Pam,' he said, moving on, 'are you coming down for the sixth?'

February 6th was the anniversary of our mother's death and there was always a family event. It was something We took for granted all through childhood, all of us did. Every year there was a gathering: all of us children – even Vincent was allowed home for it – and our mum's brother and sisters, including of course our Auntie Violet, Dad of course, and his mother, our nan, and sometimes his brothers too. Some neighbours came, friends who knew what it was all about. I remember those occasions in glimpses; I wouldn't be able to tell you what order they came in. They were partly sombre, with our mother's photograph displayed with a black ribbon on it and a red rose because of her name. It was a studio photo, taken just before she was married, a thin and pretty woman then, unwilling to smile too broadly, wearing a floral dress and a necklace of pretend pearls. If We ever tried to reconstruct some memory of her We always thought of her in that dress, slender, with those pearls, and that slightly anxious half-smile on her face, even though We knew from our siblings that she died as a well-built, big-bosomed woman, a hardworking matriarch, mother of eight.

The beginning of the evening was people arriving, and speaking quietly to each other about her, and about other people who had died. But later in the evening – and as We grew older We were allowed to stay later – there was drinking and people began talking of other things, and smiling, and telling stories, and jokes, and calling across the room to each other. I don't mean that there was music and dancing, only that the job was done, so to speak, the job of remembering and being sad, and everyone could get on with their lives.

I looked at my calendar, though I already knew.

'I would,' I said, 'you know I would, but it's a Tuesday. No way I can get off work.'

'Not even an afternoon?' He had absolutely no idea how schools have to be run.

'Not even that,' I said. 'And even if I could, how would I get back for the next morning?' We had had this conversation so many times with our brothers and sisters.

'That's a point,' he said. 'After drinking and everything. Still I thought I'd ask. You know we always like to see you. What about the next holidays?'

'I would,' I said again. 'But Heidi and me – there's still a lot to do. We've got to clear the house, and Heidi needs help with the kids –'

'I tell you darlin, she's lucky she's got you,' said Alan, which showed how much he knew, but made me feel a bit guilty for fobbing him off with less than half a truth.

People were kind, I knew that. Annoying, but on the whole, kind. I had various tentative offers of company – If you feel up to it, they'd say, or, I don't know if you'd like to – but no, I didn't like to. I still don't.

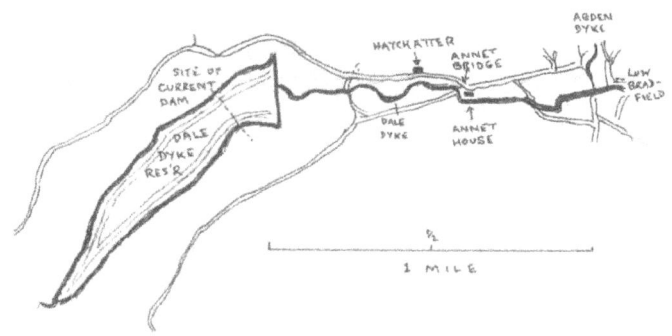
After Alan's phone call, without thinking what I was going to do, I drove to Low Bradfield and walked up to the dam again. For a change it was not raining – it had rained a lot that month and the roads were running with water and the ditches were overflowing. But at times the sun threatened to force its way through the cloud. I walked up the road, a quiet, tree-lined road. A flock of fieldfares was grazing in a field, and little birds were beginning to cheep a bit, as if rehearsing for spring.

The dam was peaceful, massive, reassuringly solid looking. At its further edge excess water was running down the spillway. Beside the path a small stone with the letters CLOB carved in it marks the centre line of the original bank, and a notice board gives you the briefest of information. A tiny plaque is the only memorial for the dead.

As I was about to turn away from the dam the clouds moved and the sun shone from just above the moors to the west, turning the water from pewter to silver and shining through the bare twigs of the distant trees so that they resembled smoke.

I turned and stood and looked back at the dam, with the sun still shining on it. I tried to imagine it on a dark and stormy night, rain pelting down, and the dam wall brand new, the reservoir receiving water for the first time, and almost full. This was foolish of me, because this dam is not the original one that collapsed, but a later one, built a little way upstream on a more suitable foundation. But that's the nature of trying to look for history – there's always something changed, something less, or more. Go to a castle – do you see what its builders saw in the eleventh century? You're lucky if it has a roof. And if it does it will certainly be wired for electric light – no pathetic little rushlights here. Far better, if it's authenticity you want, to believe the words in a book.

"The crack in the dam, having been discovered, was reported to John Gunson, the chief engineer. He came out from Sheffield to examine it and was lucky not to be the first person to be swept away by the torrent. He clambered up the embankment just as six hundred and fifty million gallons of water flooded through the breach in the dam."

I tried to, but couldn't, imagine him, John Gunson, a Victorian professional man, a practical, responsible, well-thought-of man, suddenly watching the water flowing under his feet, water that should be safely the other side of his dam, disbelieving the evidence of his eyes and at the same time knowing that here was a problem, a catastrophe, a major tragedy just beginning. I tried to see him, practicality and self-preservation kicking in, getting out of the path of what he knew was just about to happen, while at the same time being unable to process the immensity of what he, more than anyone, knew what could happen next. I tried to imagine the mud on the knees of his trousers as he reached the safety of the land beside the dam, and the panic and wonder in his face when he turned round to see what was behind him. But I didn't feel anything. I knew it but I couldn't feel it, and it was clear to me that I would never feel anything again, not properly.

He got out of that night alive, though disgraced. You can see his grave in Sheffield General Cemetery.

"Annet Bridge was washed away, and so was a farmhouse, the first building in the path of the deluge. Luckily the residents had been warned of the breach in the dam and were able to escape."

Catkins hung from the trees, dogs barked as I walked past a farm and I continued, looking to my right at the river, and at High Bradfield to my left up on the hill, until I came to Low Bradfield, where I hoped to find a teashop open.

"Several houses were washed away in the village of Low Bradfield, but there was only one death. It seems that there had been rumours already that there was a problem with the dam, and the residents were already nervous and some had made plans to flee if necessary."

What a wonderful word is 'flee.' How historical-sounding, how much weightier than 'run away.' How biblical.

"Joseph Dawson, the village tailor, managed to get his brother and his little boy out of the house before the flood hit it, but his wife was confined to bed, having given birth only the day before. He tried to carry her, wrapped in blankets and holding the baby but the water forced them back into their house. They managed to get upstairs but the baby was dropped and in the dark they were unable to retrieve it from the waters. A neighbour brought a ladder to lay between their bedroom window and the hill, so that they could escape."

This used to be a crucial punctuation when I taught this subject. Sometimes I kept it in reserve until we came out to see the course of the flood, but more often I used it in class to end my first lesson on the subject. It had a grand effect. Sometimes one of the girls would even cry. If any of the boys looked like scoffing – not many ever did – I used to ask them if they thought they would be able to carry a grown woman and a day-old baby through a flood as high as their waist.

'But he was a man,' one said once. 'We're only boys.'

Which made it possible to explain how likely it was that he would have been a skinny, maybe undernourished, specimen, a poor thin tailor.

'What happened to him after?' they used to ask, but I had never researched that far and I never knew. Neither could I identify which of the cottages might be his, so I told them it was too badly damaged to rebuild. Maybe half the 'historical' facts in the world are handed on and written down on the same shaky foundation.

I also used to tell them, truthfully, how the school was swept away, which usually provoked a cheer and they liked the story of the pig who sensed something was going to happen and broke out of its sty and was found later, safe on higher ground.

Low Bradfield is a cosy, prosperous little village now, tucked into the valley, bracketed by reservoirs and centred on the cricket pitch. The Post Office was open for tea and cake and as I sat down in the corner I realised it must have been a good half hour since I had given any thought to my sister. I had been thinking more about the tailor's wife. Did she fight against being hauled upstairs and pushed out by the bedroom window, did she struggle to go back for her new baby? Did she sob for days afterwards, or did she accept it as God's will? Or both? Did the father feel guilt for failing to save the poor little thing? Did he have to justify himself, telling himself that without a wife he would not be able to bring up the children, that they could have other babies but his wife was less replaceable? Did they ever have more children? I had never thought these things before. I had believed it was all long ago and no longer mattered. I said to myself that I must be in a peculiar mood, and it would be better if I got a hold of myself.

But later, at home, I found I couldn't stop thinking about the tailor's wife, and wondering why. Why, in the study of history, why, all through school and O level and A level, all through Teacher Training College, all through years, *years*, of teaching children what happened and how, why did most of us – students and teachers – never feel an emotional response to the things that happened?

Having your home burnt to the ground by Viking invaders, having your village wiped out by the Black Death, being tortured on the rack, being beheaded, shipwrecked, banished, fleeing (that word again) across an ocean and finding there was nothing to eat there, or else dying of swamp fever. Being a soldier, a sailor, being flogged, shot at, hacked to bits. Being a woman, giving birth – I didn't like to think about it – watching your babies die – and I was back with the tailor's wife. It was as if we'd never thought of the past before as containing humans, only figures, drawings in a history book. Gone, long ago, piled up with all the rest of the anonymous dead. Or was it only me? Me, now.

Was it only me? Did other people find their eyes filling with tears on account of orphaned children, mutilated survivors of wars, chimney sweeps and infant mine-workers? They didn't, I was sure they didn't, I never did and even now I don't. Nobody can care that much; they have enough to be going on with caring about the present; there's plenty there after all to worry about, without the tailor's wife. She'd be dead now anyway, probably lived to have more children, probably wished she hadn't so many, lived to a good age, was pointed out to the end of her life as the woman who cheated the flood, whose baby was the first victim. A little bit of fame. Probably.

Next time the phone rang it turned out to be Jimmy's wife, the fancifully named Verona.

'If we moved the date,' she said, without any preamble, 'could you come on the tenth? Is that your half-term?'

I couldn't say no, could I, when they had gone to some trouble for me, so although I didn't want to go – I *really* didn't want to go – I said I would, and I said a sort of grudging thank you, and she told me a long story about who had said what to who, and who had agreed straight away, and how it wasn't going to be any trouble at all, being only family, mostly, and so on. Then she asked how I was, and how Heidi was, and whether she might come with me, and I pointed out that she had four children, and she said why not bring them, and I reminded her that one had special needs and wouldn't be able to cope with all the people, and one was a not-quite-crawling baby and would be crushed underfoot, and she started to say she was sure everyone would understand and make allowances, and I said firmly it wasn't on, not in the least and I could hear the relief in her voice when she said, never mind, maybe another time. But I thought, after she'd rung off, why shouldn't I take Jarvis.

Well, there were reasons on both sides. I would be responsible for him. It would commit me to going; I wouldn't be able to change my mind once I'd made the offer to him, and if on the way there I felt like turning back and coming home I wouldn't be able to. On the other hand it would be company for me, on the journey. It would be something for him, to meet his family, his great-aunts, his great-uncles, his cousins and, possibly, some of his cousins' children. A wider family. Because what did he have? He had his mother, a brother, a half-sister and brother, a father he rarely saw and didn't like, and me. I supposed he had friends but I'd never asked. He was a quiet, pale, considerate boy who might have one friend in school of a similar type. They'll sit together, I imagined, slightly apart from the hurly-burly, and talk geekily together about something like Superman, or Game of Thrones, or aeroplane statistics, or bus routes, something that no one else cares about. Why shouldn't I take him? Heidi would not want him to go, she would like him to be around at half-term, to help with the other children, but it was only a weekend, Gavin could put in a shift after all. I decided I would do it.

At the weekend Heidi and I started the clearing of the bungalow.

It was a dinky little house, four rooms, two bedrooms at the front and sitting room at the back, and a kitchen big enough to eat in. It was full of stuff. Like me, she owned all kinds of objects; unlike me, she kept most of them tidily in their places, and most of them had a current purpose. Even so, dealing with the volume and variety of it all would take more than one day.

I arrived there before Heidi, and stood in the front garden – paved with blocks and containing a pair of skimmias and a bay tree, in pots, all trimmed like lollipops. I assessed the front of the house. Did it need anything painted, any gutters cleaned out, any fence mended? No, because someone – *she*, my sister – kept on top of things like that; no one was more efficient when it came to home maintenance; no one had as many tradesmen that she called upon regularly, from window-cleaners to boiler technicians, hedge-cutters to car mechanics. Weekly it seemed, she told me off for letting things slide, and told Heidi off too, because Heidi was quite a bit like me in that respect.

'Heidi. Hi.' I saw the corners of her mouth twitch downwards. She hated it when I said that – which was why I did it.

She had left Jarvis at home with Jojo and Cassie, who was three, and just brought the baby, who was young enough to be contained in a buggy for some of the time at least.

However close my sister and I had been, and however often I had been in her kitchen and living room over the past fifteen years or so, I had rarely set foot in her bedroom, or the spare room. Why would I? So I was surprised and alarmed when I saw her wardrobe door standing open and clothes strewn across the bed, until I realised that I had left it that way, when I went there to get a dress for her to be buried in. *That* was because my sister Barbara had demanded to be able to see her in her coffin, though in the end she didn't feel up to it. Waste of a good black dress therefore.

My sister was more domesticated than me – obviously, she'd been trained to teach kids to cook and, in the old days, clean as well, and when We lived together, till Heidi was four or five, she took care of all that sort of thing. Then, I never needed to learn and since then I have muddled through with school dinners and ready meals and toast. It's been fine.

I moved out of living with her and Heidi a long time ago, because of a boyfriend – hers not mine. I'd saved enough money for a deposit and I was fed up with having Heidi moved into my bedroom every time some new boyfriend got to the staying over stage. So I left, Heidi got my bedroom; boyfriends, I presumed, came and went in the same fashion they always had done.

'Where shall we start?' I said, though I had no intention of allowing her to decide. 'I would suggest the kitchen.'

Naturally the kitchen was spotless, except for the dust of a few weeks. A Christmas cactus was flowering on the windowsill, but the other plants had suffered from a lack of water. I took them to my car, thinking I might save some. When I came back in Heidi was opening cupboards.

'Why don't you take the food?' I said. There were things I was *not* going to let her have, so it seemed a good idea to start by giving her what she *could* have. She rejected some of the stuff – ('The kids won't eat lentils.') – but collected the tins, and most of the contents of the freezer into boxes which I had brought from the supermarket and piled them into her car. Her mother's car actually – she hadn't waited to take possession of that.

'What about the cookery books?' I said. There was a whole shelf of them, plus a run of ring binders, matching, where she kept recipes she cut out of magazines, or made up herself. Heidi looked at me. I looked at Heidi. We tried to stop ourselves from a little snort of mirth. The idea of either of us cooking from a recipe book was laughable.

'I'll take them to school,' I said. 'There are people there who might like them.'

She did not, as I thought she might, say anything about e-bay. She was not, so far, behaving badly.

She did not want any of the clothes. There was nothing to fit her anyway, as she was taller than We were and an entirely different shape, and naturally her taste was different. I could not imagine myself dressed in any of the clothes, my taste being different as well, but I could not yet countenance taking them to a charity shop, so I bundled them into carrier bags

– many bags – and put them on the back seat of my car.

'We need to leave the furniture for now,' said Heidi. 'It's nice after all, in its way, and it will help to sell.' She was a person who watched property programmes.

But there were still cupboards to empty – kitchenware and tablecloths, bedding and books and cleaning materials, and there was still some way to go when Heidi's phone rang. It was Jarvis. I could hear the sound of screaming.

'I need to go,' said Heidi to me. 'He can't get Cassie to eat anything and she's screaming and she's setting Jojo off. Honestly – Jarv. He's nearly fifteen, you'd think he'd be able to cope for an hour or two.'

'You ask too much of that boy,' I said, and she rolled her eyes because she'd heard it too many times before.

'I'll stay and do some more,' I said.

'Anything electrical,' she said, '– leave it for today. There's things I need.'

'Fine,' I said. I was not bothered about CD players and the like.

When she was gone the house felt emptier – because it was emptier – and if I had been the right sort of person I might have felt a ghostly presence. It would have been welcome. But it no longer looked like her house; too much had been taken out; all the little things, the magazines under the TV, the shoes from the hallway, the house plants from the windowsill, the calendar on the wall, the photos of the children magneted to the fridge, the post-it notes by the phone. There was nothing to show that a real person had ever lived here.

I went into her bedroom again. Heidi had taken the duvet and bed linen and we had kept just one counterpane to cover the bare bed. She'd dumped all the jars of moisturiser and hand cream and the lipsticks and mascara into a bag so the dressing table was bare too. Tidy and cold.

I opened the hatch and pulled down the loft ladder. She would never go up there herself unless I was in the house with her – 'If I fall down and break a leg I want someone here to call an ambulance.' Yes, well.

She kept her loft as tidy as her house. No bulging plastic bags here, no scruffy cardboard boxes, no broken artefacts just dumped by the hatch waiting to be tripped over. Her excess belongings were in labelled boxes, stacked on shelves. Lesson plans. Christmas decorations. Curtain hooks. Her matching luggage, one large suitcase, one small, tucked into a corner near the hatch for easy access. Spare pillows. Jam jars.

It would have to be cleared, I knew that, but not just then. I would wait for Heidi to be in the house with me.

And now here I am, in 2020, in Pauline's house. Bungalow. Living here, having lived here now for years. Still not used to it. Still with her ghost at odd times, these days even more often, now that I can't go out.

I look out of her window, not mine – it's never a busy street, but now it's as if we have been invaded by aliens and vaporised. Occasional joggers, some of them looking very much like lockdown starters; the occasional neighbour with some shopping. I am not acquainted with the neighbours, although Pauline was. In spite of all the publicity about the kindness of friends and neighbours, none of them have asked me if I need so much as a pint of milk. I do, as it happens, but I have taken to drinking my tea without. I'm used to it now.

One of my neighbours walks past my window, sees me, does a minimal nod. It wouldn't hurt you, I think, to smile. What if it did though? What if someone correlated the catching of the virus with having been the recipient of a random smile from a stranger, a neighbour, a niece or nephew? Would we have to stop doing it? Would we be *able* to stop doing it? These are the stupid sorts of thoughts that go through a person's head when they have too much solitude.

Even at my lowest, in the first months after Pauline's death, I found my face doing social smiles even when it was far from what I wanted it to be doing. They may not have been convincing smiles, maybe not sincere – in fact, certainly not sincere; but they happened, in spite of my true feelings, and as time passed became less and less unnatural.

Phone call from Alan. He still calls me nearly every day, whenever he has some bad news to impart. Alison is not feeling well, she thinks she may have touched a trolley in Sainsbury's without her gloves on. Olive and Verona *say* they're all right, but are they really?

They have each other, and enough food to last out a medieval siege, I tell him. And then there's Barbara, he says. She's over eighty, she misses Maureen, her daughters don't seem to do much for her. What about me, I think. I haven't even got any daughters. *You* might be locked down, I think, but *I* am a step further on; *I* am in quarantine.

The beginning of February, before we broke, not a moment too soon, for half-term, saw us returning to school – or staying late – for what used to be called Parents' Evening but was now, after much argument and pondering, called Consultation Evening, which made us sound like doctors.

I sat behind a table, with my name on it, and waited for the parents and, theoretically, the students who were in my form as well as those who were taking GCSE History. I was to tell them how close they were to being on course and up to date with all their work, and give them some idea of their expected grades. The parents' job was to understand and undertake to support their offspring by monitoring their homework and their revision and impressing on them the importance of these exams. I knew it was all humbug and so did some of the parents – the ones that didn't know just went away depressed and defeated by the task, unless – like the mothers of Kane and Josh – they had chosen not to come at all.

I did see Daisy's mother though. I noticed them doing the rounds of all the other subjects – Daisy towering over her mother by a good six inches – but when it came to be my turn, right at the end, my last appointment and also theirs, her mother sent her to wait outside the hall.

She was a nice woman, older than most mothers, her hair grey and her eyes tired. I knew that Daisy's father was not a presence in their lives, and never had been; I also knew that there was an established stepfather figure who on previous occasions had come along with her, but this night she was on her own.

'I'm concerned about Daisy,' I said. Concerned is the thing to be, rather than exasperated or irritated.

'I know,' she said. 'I don't know, I've tried – she won't talk to me, she's never at home, she –'

'She's often late for school,' I said. 'That wouldn't matter so much if she –'

'I can't get her out of bed in the mornings,' she said.

'She should be having a good night's sleep,' I said. It was fatuous, I knew as I said it. This woman knew just as much, and more, about her daughter as I did. And I wasn't in a position to preach about a good night's sleep for when did I ever have one, unless it was helped on by whisky.

'Her friends,' said her mother. 'Her old friends just aren't around any more. I don't know where she's going in the evenings, or who she's with. I'm so worried. But she's sixteen, I can't stop her going out and to be honest, it's a relief when she's out, it's all so –'

'Difficult time for teenagers,' I said. Fatuous again.

'Well, I know,' she said. 'But it's also – my partner, he's ill – heart – waiting for an operation, can't work, home all day worrying, bored. I'm out at work, I'm worrying too, about him, then about Daisy. She won't talk about it, won't talk about anything, except to argue when I try – I just can't get near her.' She rubbed her eyes with the back of her hand. 'I'm sorry,' she said. 'I know I should be talking about her predicted grades, but they don't seem to be very important at the moment, not when we might lose Tony, and I even fear – I try not to think it – I could lose Daisy as well.'

I did not need this. I was aware of my limitations, at the best of times, in the comfort and counselling departments of life; I should have been able to wear a badge saying, Get your sympathy somewhere else, then maybe this poor woman would not have been looking hopefully at me.

'She used to say she wanted to be a doctor,' she said. 'I've been putting money by for years for her to go to university, I was so proud of her, Tony was too. Now I just see horrible futures for her.'

Heidi came into my mind. We – her mother and I – had had those fears and those conversations about the awful possible futures. It only made me feel more helpless to help.

'Look,' I said. 'She will get some grades, she's clever. Even if she doesn't revise she'll get something.' That was pretty much off-message. 'Even if she doesn't get a GCSE at all she can go to the sixth form college and retake them. And you might find out, in the future, that they're not – GCSEs – all that important really.' That was *really* off-message. 'Honestly,' I said, 'I sometimes meet ex-pupils that I thought were going to end up in *prison* and I find they've got jobs and babies, and a house and a dog. You know – normal.'

That was the best I could do, and she knew it. If she had had hopes of me, well, she didn't any more. I gave her a schedule of revision sessions and an exam timetable and she went away and I put my head down on my rickety table and wished I could have a good cry, there and then instead of waiting till bedtime.

'Coming to the pub?' said Frank Midgeley as we assisted the caretaker to stack the chairs.

'No thanks,' I said. 'Too tired.' But later, at home on my own, I wished I had said yes.

Even Heidi had been to the February event on a couple of occasions when she was a child, but not at all since Jojo was a baby. Jarvis had never been south to visit. He knew that he had a number of cousins and even more second cousins – if that is what your cousins' children are properly called – who still, mostly, lived in Essex, but they were as distant to him as his (almost non-existent) father's family.

We were setting off on Friday after school and we were going to sleep two nights at Maureen's. Heidi had not been pleased at all, I knew, but I didn't care. 'Your mother would have taken him,' I said to her. 'She would approve.'

The rain in Sheffield looked set to turn to snow, but as we moved further south it confined itself to a thin drizzle. Jarvis was very quiet in the car as we drove through the dark; I almost expected him to ask to be taken home again and I wondered what I would do when he did.

'Shall I tell you what this is all about?' I said to him.

'All right,' he said.

'I'm not sure where to start,' I said. 'You must know some of this already. You've heard about the flood?'

'Sort of,' he said.

'It was 1953,' I said. He said nothing. 'It was huge,' I said. 'It was a massively high tide, all round the coast – you know, don't you, not everywhere gets a high tide at the same time?'

'No,' he said.

'Well, it's true. So, say high tide is eight o'clock somewhere, say in Scotland, then further south it won't be high tide till, say nine o'clock.'

'Oh,' he said.

'So this high tide, along with really strong storm winds – gales, you know – I think a ship was sunk somewhere, maybe on the west coast, and this tide, this storm surge, just continued round the top of Scotland and all the way down the east coast, right down to where we lived then.'

'Where you lived. On that island, right?'

Our mum Rose Corner, was born on Canvey Island. She married our dad, Edward Dearly in 1931 and they had eight children. There was Eddie and Jimmy, twins, then Maureen, then Barbara, then Vincent. No children were born to her during the war but when our dad came home for good they had Alan and then us.

We – by which I mean me and my twin sister – had no memories of our mother. Our last sight of her was of her being carried away by flood water, but We couldn't remember it, however hard We tried. We were being carried, in the dark, through the sea water, by Barbara and Maureen; our dad carried Alan who was five. Our oldest brothers were away doing their national service, or things might have turned out differently. Our mum was holding Vin by the collar and carrying a cardboard box containing all the family birth certificates and the insurance policy and the child allowance book and what was left of the last week's wages. No one knows which of them, either Vinny or our mother, lost their footing. The packages they were holding were dropped into the cold sea and both of them, the stout woman and the skinny boy were swept away from the rest of us.

I tell him this.

'Which one carried Granma?'

'Which –?'

'Maureen or Barbara?'

'We don't know. They couldn't remember. It was lucky, you know, that Maureen was even there. She didn't live at home any more – she was married, with a baby. She heard the weather was going to be bad and she came across to the island to tell my Mum to come over to hers for the night.'

'Why didn't she phone?'

'Nobody had phones then –'

'I know they didn't have mobiles –'

'People like us didn't have a phone at all. Anyway, she left the baby – Nicky that was – with her next door neighbour and came across and she says our mum said she'd be all right, but then our dad came home from work early and said they all had to get across, off the island. And our mum really didn't want to, she wanted to stay in the house. I don't remember all this of course, it's what I've been told.'

'And she got drowned. I know that much,' he said.

'They pulled her out of the water before she actually drowned –'

'Who did?'

'Some men in a boat. Emergency services I suppose. Or maybe just people using a boat to get to safety – I don't know.'

'So she was still alive?'

'Oh yes. She went to the hospital and died later. Six days later.'

We never saw Mum again. The older ones did – Eddie and Jim were allowed leave especially to see her, lying in bed with double pneumonia, but little children were not allowed to visit, not us, not even Alan. Vin was in hospital too and recovered, up to a point. Didn't die at least.

The big age gap in our family between Vincent, the fifth child, and Alan, the sixth was because of the war. Vin was only a few weeks old when it started and our dad, who worked at the oil refinery on Canvey Island, was needed in the shipyards because he was a boilermaker and many of the young men were going into the navy. I understood from my older siblings that he sometimes came home on leave from Glasgow where he was building and repairing ships, but it was only when the war ended that he came back home properly and went back to work at the refinery.

(I remember overhearing two kids talking in the classroom – 'What's the most boring thing in the world?' 'Teachers telling you about the second world war.')

Alan was born in 1947, and three years later, We were born. We always knew that there had been a time before the flood when We lived with our mum and dad, and Alan and Vin, and our sisters Maureen and Barbara, and our brothers Jimmy and Eddie when they came home on leave. We knew it but We didn't remember it. We only remembered living in our Nan's house in South Benfleet, and later our Auntie Vi's in Leigh-on-Sea. After the flood.

Our two sisters both married very young. A lot of girls did in those days, having, maybe, nothing better to look forward to. And I suppose that, like my sisters, many of them were pregnant. Maureen was the first of the family to get married and our nephew Nicky was born before We were two years old. Before. Barbara too was only seventeen when she married Brian the year after the flood. After. She lost the baby though and that, coming so soon After, is believed in the family to have done her no good.

Eddie got married to Olive and We were bridesmaids, four years old, in pink net with little wreaths on our heads of artificial flowers, which would not stay straight but slipped over our eyes in a drunken way. The church hall where the reception was held was full of unknown children it seemed, and thin young men in suits and big-bosomed women in full-skirted dresses. Vin, allowed home for the event, stood uncertainly near Auntie Vi, who was our mum's sister and looked a bit like her. We found that our silver sandals, bought especially for the day, had smooth soles that enabled us to slide up and down the floor. We persuaded Alan to take his shoes off and slide with us, in his socks. When we managed to collide with and flatten Maureen's Nicky someone or other remonstrated with us. One of the aunties I suppose, or just some busybody. She was giving Alan a proper scolding, including, 'You're his uncle, you're supposed to look after him, not knock him down like skittles.'

We thought about this. We had thought that uncle meant grown-up. We had some uncles – they were the fatter men in tight suits who were standing near the beer. We asked Auntie Vi.

'Alan's an uncle, and you two are aunties.'

'Auntie what?' said one of us.

'Auntie Pam and Auntie Pauline.'

Pauline. That was her name.

Soon after this Jimmy married Verona, who was Olive's sister and We wore our silver sandals again, this time with lemon net dresses.

From then on it seemed We were always being taken to see a new baby, or to a birthday party, or to see a nephew or more often a niece in a Sunday school play or a dancing display. None of them lived more than a bus ride away so even Nan could take us, although We liked it better when our dad came to get us, in his Sunday suit, and We could sit on the top deck of the bus and he would give us money for sweets when he went away, after taking us back to Nan's and telling her over a cup of tea all about where We had been, and making her laugh.

The brother We rarely saw was Vincent. He had gone to live in some special boarding school at the seaside. Canvey was the seaside of course, but there you breathed in whatever it was that came out of the refinery chimneys so it wasn't bracing in the way that Norfolk apparently was. Vin had a weak chest, made worse by being nearly drowned by the flood, and died young, his health not improved by heavy smoking and not having a wife to look after him. Said my sisters.

'So this party,' I said, 'is something that has happened every year – I think every year – since the flood. It's in honour of our mum, but not only that –'

'What else?'

I realised I didn't really know.

'I suppose,' he said, 'it's just about getting the family all together.'

'That's a very good way of putting it,' I said, sounding like the schoolteacher I am.

'Like they all came to Granma's funeral.'

'Just like that.'

'So the really old man? That doddery one?'

'Eddie,' I said. 'He's not that old.'

'How old?'

I worked it out. 'Seventy-four this year. Jimmy's the same. Twins.'

'That *is* really old.'

'To you it is. They've only recently retired. They used to have amusement arcades – you know, slot machines. They did pretty well.'

'They haven't got them now?' he said, hopefully.

'Sold them,' I said. 'None of the family wanted to take them on.'

'I would've,' he said. 'They should have asked me.'

He sat quietly, contemplating his missed opportunity I suppose, while I negotiated the roundabout on to the A1.

'And Barbara and Maureen will be there,' I said. 'Remember them? And Alan. And all their wives and husbands.'

'Am I going to be the only young person?' he said. We had already had this conversation.

'There's always kids there,' I said. 'Not that your mum's cousins are kids any more – she's one of the youngest, obviously, but they always bring some of their young ones. And *their* young ones have young ones. Don't ask me their names, or who belongs to who, though. Some of them are bound to be around your age. Honestly, it will be all right.'

'So it won't be like a funeral?'

'Honestly. I wouldn't be going myself if it was like that.'

'But you don't always go?'

'It's a long way. It hasn't always been convenient. They used to have it on February sixth, no alternative allowed, so We only could go – your Granma and I – when it fell on a weekend. But they're a bit more relaxed about it now. That's why they've changed it this time. They know it's hard for people when they're at work and have busy lives, to travel and have a big do midweek.'

'I guess,' he said, and fell to considering again. 'Have I to call them Auntie?'

'It would be best,' I said. 'Then it won't matter if you forget their names.'

'Maureen and Barbara,' he said.

'And Olive and Verona and Alison. But don't fret – Auntie will do fine.'

'Maureen and Barbara,' he said again. 'Are they twins too?'

'No. In fact they don't even get on together that well. They start to argue after about five minutes in each other's company, about the slightest little thing.'

'Oh,' he said. 'Like you and Granma.'

I glanced at him, but he wasn't trying to be clever, or nasty – two things he's hardly capable of.

'What makes you think that?'

He fidgeted a bit. 'Mum says no one would think you were twins. Granma was kind –' he stopped to hear what he had just said. 'No, I mean, you're kind too, but different. If you know what I mean.'

'I know what you mean,' I said. 'You mean your Granma was soft. She liked to spoil everyone.'

'Even you?' He said it as if it was a new idea to him.

'I suppose you could say that. Even me. But someone has to have a firm grip, else where would we be?'

'I don't know,' he said, whispering.

I drove on, south down the A1 through the dark and the drizzle, I thought of how I had allowed her name to pass through my brain, when I remembered the silver sandals. Pauline. I allowed it again. And mine began with the same letter. When We were little We would readily answer to either name and until We went to school We were unable to really grasp that We were two separate people. Separate people, but the same. The same but two separate people, the big people explained to us but We never entirely believed it. We knew it but We didn't feel it.

We were the same. We came from the same act of intercourse. We were together from being a blastocyst. We had the same mother and father, the same brothers and sisters. We looked the same, same straw-y hair, same sea-grey eyes. We slept together in the same twin pram; We sat near the table in our separate highchairs, helping ourselves from each other's tray, patting our little hands in each other's spilled milk. We had the same earliest memory, of being stung by wasps, both of us on the lips, possibly by the same wasp but possibly not, while eating ice cream cornets in our nan's back yard. We were brought up by the same people, first our mother and father, then our nan, and then by Auntie Vi.

We were in the same class all through infant and junior school, We sat together, We put our hands up at the same time, We chanted our tables in the same key. We looked identical but our teachers knew which one was which because she was left-handed and sat on my left so as not to bump arms. (Later in life I was always puzzled about that left-handedness. Why should there be that difference? But then I reminded myself that We were two halves of one egg, so one of us – her? – must have been the left-hand side.)

We had the same friends, girls We went to school with and played with in the street, but I don't think there was ever a time when one of us went off to play without the other one. We would not have been able to think of such a thing. We wore the same size shoes, We were the same height, the same weight. We had the same illnesses at the same time, measles, chicken pox, mumps and German measles; both of us in bed in a darkened room – that was the measles; both of us scratching in spite of a covering of calamine lotion when We had chicken pox. We slept in the same bed until we were thirteen, the same room until We were eighteen, and even after that We were in the same hall of residence, with only a thin wall between us.

Even our disagreements, squabbles, quarrels, whatever – they were always started with the prospect of being apart. Say We were out playing. One of us might want to go indoors but the other one could not let her go and be left – not alone for there would be other people out to play with, but without the other half. Or, say one of us said they liked a song – the other one had the choice of liking it too, just as much, *or* persuading her that it was an awful song, that nobody could like it. Same with people, friends, actors, singers, groups; same with films and TV programmes, and food, and clothes. It took us a long time to learn to tolerate the other's preferences if they were different from our own. 'Our own' was a concept We hardly had. And it wasn't really tolerance – We only pretended, so as to stay as what We were: one.

'So you went to live with your Granma?'

He knew We did, he was only trying to get me back into a conversation with him.

'Our nan,' I said.

Our nan, our dad's mum that is, took us three youngest to live with her. Alan was five and We were two and a half. She must have been well over sixty at the time, which is no joke when you have to, without warning or preparation, take responsibility for three small children, bereaved and bewildered and given to wetting the bed. She got through it by letting us play out with other kids at all hours of the day and evening, and feeding us sugar sandwiches when we cried.

'She was too old to be doing it really,' I said. 'But there was nobody else. There weren't nurseries then where you could leave your children. Alan went to school but We were under her feet all day. It was hard work for her – all the washing – she didn't have a washing machine and We played out and got mucky –'

'You played out?' he said. 'Before you were even old enough to go to school? Where? Where did you play?'

'In the street. There wasn't much traffic to worry about. Nan could look out of her front window and see if We were all right.'

'What did you play with?'

'I don't know. Whatever was lying around I suppose. When the big children came home from school they let us play with them. Sometimes.'

'But you could get lost. Or someone could come and abduct you.'

I shrugged. 'Someone would find us. And no one would want to abduct us I'm sure, grubby little urchins that We were.'

'Cassie never goes outside by herself,' he said.

'Things are different now,' I told him.

'I know,' he said. 'You've told me. Did your nan hit you?'

We were never hit, not properly, not what our nan called a good hiding. Sometimes, if We were cheeky we got what she called a clip round the ear, but mostly We got away with it. Alan came off worse because he was a boy – at least he would have done if she had been able to catch him, or hold on to him. But though she never hurt him, he came in for a lot of casual scuffs and swipes, with whatever she was holding in her hand. If it was just a dishcloth he was lucky; once it was the coal shovel. He loved her though, more than We did, and later refused to come and live with us at Auntie Vi's, staying with Nan until he found her dead one day in her chair when he came home from work.

'She was pretty nice to us,' I said.

Maureen levered herself out of my car and ushered us into Eddie's rather palatial house as if she owned us. (Jim and Eddie, it should be said, had done well for themselves in the slot machine arcade business. While it was true that Canvey wasn't the holiday destination it once had been, people were still coming for days out and they had been able to sell their beeping, buzzing, flashing dens for tidy sums when they retired.)

In the hall a pair of teenagers – grandchildren of someone I guessed – took our coats. In the big room, that they always called the party room, they must have heard us arrive and we found them struggling out of the deep settees and on to their feet. We Dearlys have a tendency to be short in the leg and square in the shoulders, and a gathering of us, with our light brown hair now white or grey, had the look of a small flock of sheep. Olive, as the lady of the house, stood there ready to welcome us. She reached up to put her hands on Jarvis' shoulders and looked at him searchingly before she kissed him and sighed sentimentally.

'Give over,' I wanted to say. 'She wasn't *your* sister.' But I kept it in.

Barbara got herself with some effort out of a very squashy sofa and came and hugged me. When it had gone on as long as I could stand I must have stiffened because she let go quite abruptly, and turned to do the same to Jarvis. He was behaving better than I was.

Jim and Eddie sat together on the furthest settee, looking, with their little white beards, like a pair of identical garden gnomes. They stood up to greet me and then I could tell which was which because Jimmy was limping on account of a hip replacement. Apart from that they looked in fine shape, pink and smiling and satisfied with their role as joint heads of such a large family, well-off and generous, holding us all together, keeping the memories alive.

'I'm sorry,' Jim said to me. 'I'm so sorry about the funeral. Gutted. Really. But I was only just out of hospital. Couldn't do a thing for meself. So Verona couldn't leave me could she? But you know I would have if I could.'

He'd said all this to me multiple times before, and I said so.

'Have to tell you again,' he said. 'In person. Just so you know I was thinking of you. All day I was thinking of you. Wasn't I Rona?'

'He was in tears,' said Verona loyally. 'He couldn't help it, could you Jim.'

'So how is the hip?' I said. I was not that interested in the surgical details, but hoped it would get him away from his script.

'Fine,' he said. 'And all the better for seeing you. It's a few years isn't it, since you've managed to get down for it.'

I always thought this year on year insistence on our little family tragedy was guilt on the part of Jimmy and Eddie, for not being there at the time of the flood. They were away doing their National Service, it was not their fault or their wish to be somewhere else, bashing about on Salisbury Plain, far from the sea, but they knew things would have been different if they had been at home. And our dad, when he was alive, and more and more the older he got, made their guilt worse by getting upset.

'She didn't want to leave,' he used to say, always late on in the evening when he moved on from beer to Scotch. 'She wanted to climb on the roof and wait. It could have worked out all right. I knew some people who got away with it.'

And one of the older ones would say, 'Yes, and you knew some people who died doing it. You did the best you knew.'

'I should have had a rope,' he would say. 'I should have roped us all together.'

And Ed or Jim would say, 'You didn't have no rope though, did you?'

'In the shed there might have been some.'

And they would say, 'Dad, the shed had already gone hadn't it? Washed away, you told us.'

And Barbara would say, 'That's right Dad. We saw it just break up and float round the yard. That was when we thought we'd better get out. Remember?'

'If I'd have got home sooner –'

'Dad –'

'If I'd have gone in after her –'

But how could he? He had five of his children almost safe. It wasn't possible to put Alan down. Maureen and Barbara had their hands full of us. They could only watch Rose and Vin floundering and splashing in the water, and shout to them, and hold out a spare hand as if it would help.

These conversations used to make people cry, and Olive would offer more whisky as a diversion. I think that after Dad died we gave up crying at these gatherings. But still, this time, there was our mother's picture on the sideboard, as usual, with the red rose in a tasteful small vase beside it. Less prominent but there too was one of our dad, square on to the camera and smiling broadly, and a smaller one of Vinny, blurred and a bit ghostly but the only picture of him we ever saw. These were what we had all seen before. What I wasn't prepared for was a framed picture of *her* – of Pauline, wearing shorts, sitting on the grass in someone's garden. She looked about nineteen and I wondered why I had never seen it before until it came to me that I had, and that it was once a picture of both of us, me and her, and that someone had therefore cut me away from the photo.

It was neatly done: an old photo scanned and enhanced and trimmed and reprinted. The two of us, back from college, in Leigh-on-Sea for the summer, sitting on Vi's lawn laughing at our brother Alan as he struggled with his new fancy camera. And now I was removed as if it was me that had died; removed, except that you could still, if you knew it was there, see the edge of my knee in the bottom corner of the shot.

Since the funeral – which was less than two months before and still an unexamined memory, like an injury under a bandage which you are afraid to take off – since then I had not looked at a photo of her. Even looking at myself in the bathroom mirror as I flossed my teeth made me think of her. As did everything.

As I was recalling Alan and his camera we all heard the front door opening again.

'That will be Alan and Alison,' pronounced Olive, and she was right.

We waited, hearing the business of taking off coats and hanging them up and then they were in the room, intercepted by Olive. 'And Bradley too,' she cried, as if it was unexpected, as Bradley, the youngest of all that generation but surely by now old enough not to be trailing after his parents, slid into the room.

Alison reached my part of the room after she had submitted to being welcomed by everyone else. She and I made no attempt to kiss and/or hug.

'And this is?' she said.

'Jarvis,' I said. 'Heidi's boy. My nephew. Great nephew.'

'Jarvis,' she said, as if the name was distasteful to her. I imagined that she might try to influence the names given to her grandchildren; I imagined she might succeed.

'And how is Heidi? Coping?'

Not, how was I?

Verona came in then, from the dining room where she and her daughters had been laying out the spread, and all the hugging and kissing started all over again. When she got to Jarvis she only patted his arm and said, 'You don't want to be in here with all the old people. Come with me, I'll show you where the kids are. They're watching DVDs. You come too Pam, so you know where to find him.' I couldn't stop myself from liking Verona.

We went through the dining room. There was a table full of food, another loaded with drink. There were people all over the room, Eddie's daughters and the wives of Jim's sons bustling about, trying to fit more dishes on the table, rearranging each other's efforts, apparently without arguments. Even on that short appearance we had to stop several times to say hello, to introduce Jarvis, to be offered drinks.

Verona led us to the conservatory where on beanbags and cushions was a pile of bodies – teenagers to small ones, the various grandchildren of Janice and Sandra and Karen and Stuart, of Nicky and Julie and Madeline, of Natalie and Mel, of Chris and Michael and Gary and Tim and Greg, the children of my nephews and nieces, all of them procreating away, except, so far, for George and Bradley who would no doubt get round to it before long. I had never managed to fully grasp the names of their husbands and wives, especially now that some of them were on a second or third one, and as for their grandchildren – all those Daniels and Olivias – even if I had wanted to try there was no way I could remember their names or distinguish one from another.

The kids were watching Pirates of the Caribbean and checking out each other's phones and helping themselves to paper plates full of food from the table in the corner. There was already a significant amount on the floor.

'You'll have some clearing up to do,' I said.

'No problem,' she said. 'Me and Olive will sort it all out tomorrow. We'll have plenty of help.'

Somebody shuffled along to make room for Jarvis. Somebody else advised him to get stuck in to the pizza before it all went. I followed Verona into the dining room to meet Janice and Sandra and Karen again and say some appropriate things. I missed Jarvis hovering at my shoulder and already I longed for the evening to end.

Before too long had passed, however, it was time for the serious bit of the evening. The children were hauled out of their lair and made to gather with everyone else in the party room for Eddie's few words. It wasn't much, more of a toast than a speech. He spoke first about Pauline, and what he said I did not want to hear and concentrated hard on the sight of Alan failing to hold back his tears. He might do as he liked but I was not up for crying in public.

Eddie moved on to mention Vinny, and this time there were murmurs of agreement and approval. Then he talked of our dad and Maureen chimed in with her usual anecdote about his coming back home after the war. We weren't born at that time so it meant nothing to me. Finally, he said his usual bit about our mother – wonderful woman, devoted etc, we all had our own memories – well, We didn't, and neither did most of the other people in the room, but he said it anyway. Then we raised our glasses to their memories and Eddie sat down. The younger generation stopped fidgeting and went back to their DVD, and people drifted into the dining room to get at the food.

Alan came over to me, mopping his face with one of Olive's paper napkins.

'All right Pammy?'

'Yes,' I said.

'You're so brave,' he said. 'I'm a soft old devil I know. Don't take much to make me blub. And I don't get any better the older I get. But you manage to put a brave face on.'

Shut up, I thought. I had to ask him about his kids and grandkids to make him talk about something else.

Then Barbara pushed in between us so that she could make a fuss of him and encourage him to cry a bit more.

'For Christ sake,' I said. 'It's sixty years ago. Let him get over it.' His own wife, I should say, was keeping well out of it.

Barbara turned away from Alan and towards me; she gripped my arm, which is something I have never liked. 'It's not your fault,' she said. 'I know that and I do try to take it into consideration, but Pamela, you shouldn't be so hard. It's not good for you.'

'Fat lot you care,' I said.

'That's what I mean,' she said. 'It's only yourself that gets hurt.'

I thought she looked pretty hurt herself but then, she can cry at will when she puts her mind to it.

'You're my little sister,' she said. 'You can't get away from it. And I love you whether you like it or not. I didn't carry you through the floodwater –' Here we go, I thought '– only to fall out with you now you need me.'

'You don't know that,' I said. 'You always say that, but you don't know. It can just as well have been Maureen that carried me.'

'Does it matter?' she said.

'No,' I said. 'It's you that brings it up every time, as if it does matter. If it was you, then I wish you'd dropped me.' I did wish that, at that moment. I wished I was dead and I knew that all my family wished I was too, instead of *her*. I wasn't wanted here. I was the wrong twin, they all wished it was *her*, Pauline, that was here and that it was me who was safely reduced to ashes.

Alan took me by the elbow – another thing I don't like – and led me away. 'You're upset,' he said.

'Very perceptive I'm sure,' I said. A small part of my brain was watching all this with interest and wondering if I would be embarrassed and sorry tomorrow.

Maureen talked quietly to Jarvis as I drove back to her house. She showed him to a sofa bed in the front room and said to me that I was in the back bedroom, next to the bathroom and did I need anything. It felt to me that she was sympathetic but tired and I went to bed gratefully and slept better than I usually did. In the morning she brought a mug of tea and put it on the bedside table without saying anything.

When I went downstairs she was sitting at the breakfast table waiting for us. 'Shall I go and wake Jarvis?' I said.

'Not yet,' she said.

I sat down.

'You need to get a hold of yourself,' she said to me. 'Now that Pauline isn't here to make you mind your manners, you have to – well, as I say, you have to get a grip of yourself.'

I was not going to get into an argument so I ignored her and put a Weetabix in my bowl.

'It's no good ignoring me,' she said as if she was talking to a child. 'You can't go round upsetting people just for the fun of it. Barbara's your sister.'

I must have made a sort of snorting noise because she got more cross.

'Don't laugh,' she said. 'It's not funny. I know she can be annoying –'

'Can be!'

'Everyone's annoying some of the time –'

'You're telling me they are –'

'Pammy, listen to yourself. You sound like a little child. I'm saying this because you're my little sister and I want you to be happy.'

'I'll never be happy,' I said, and thought to myself that now I really did sound like one of those huffy girls out of Year Nine.

'I hope,' she said,' that you can call Barbara and tell her you're sorry for whatever you said to her.'

'She shouldn't get so upset,' I said. 'It was nothing.'

We could hear Jarvis moving about in the next room, and heard him going upstairs to the bathroom.

'You're not the only one with troubles,' said Maureen. 'How do you think I feel?'

Her husband Dennis was in a care home now, a once fierce and funny man reduced to sitting on a plastic cushion watching daytime TV.

'How is Dennis?' I said, though I knew she had told me the day before.

'Don't try to change the subject,' she said.

'That's enough,' I said, fed up at last. 'Stop picking on me. Leave me alone.'

'Someone has to tell you,' she said. 'I've got grandchildren – for goodness sake, I've got great-grandchildren – who can control themselves better than you when it comes to having a polite conversation. Pauline wouldn't let you get away with it so why should I.'

'You're not Pauline,' I said. My nose was running and I needed a tissue but I couldn't stop arguing long enough to look for one. A drip of snot fell into my Weetabix and Maureen handed me a box of tissues. Nicely timed, I thought, you could have noticed a bit sooner.

I blew my nose as Jarvis came into the room and Maureen said no more to me but began fussing over him, what did he like for breakfast? Did he want tea? Or coffee? Or juice? How did he sleep? Was he warm enough? Did he enjoy the party? Which she had already discussed with him on the way home the night before and didn't need to do again. I did not point this out though.

Our journey north was quieter than the southward one. We were tired, I suppose, and each of us going over, silently, the events of the previous evening.

After a long silence he said, 'Who's feeding Violet?'

'Who?' I said, and then, 'Oh Violet. I just call her the cat. Lady two doors down.' I was lying; I had actually just locked the cat out of the house, with a bowl of food in the back garden. Jarvis shouldn't know this, but if he found out I would tell him cats manage just fine on their own. They do don't they?

We were quiet again for a long way.

When we stopped at a Little Chef I made an effort.

'All right?'

'All right.'

He stirred the cream into his hot chocolate, looked out at the car park and seemed to make up his mind to start a conversation.

'Those brothers? Those old men? I wish I could have a place with games and slots and things.'

'It's just a job,' I said. 'They don't get – they didn't I mean – get to play on the machines themselves. Probably didn't even want to. It was a job. Sweeping up, keeping the machines in working order, getting things mended when they break –'

'Counting the money,' he said.

'Well yes,' I said. 'They did all right out of it. They must have saved up to get started though, to get their first place. It was only little I think. I don't know if We ever saw it.'

'They got the money off their dad,' said Jarvis. 'Barbara – Auntie Barbara – told me.'

'I never knew that,' I said. 'Your Granma and I, We never knew that.'

'She said he was a gambler, your dad, back when it was illegal, and he did the football pools as well, and he won a big load of money and he gave it to everyone in the family.'

Nearly everyone, I thought.

I did not call Barbara when I got home. I replayed in my head the things that Maureen said to me, but I did not call Barbara, and she did not call me. After a few days I sent a text to her which said simply 'Sorry,' and she did not reply, being stubborn as well as annoying. I thought – I'd thought it before – that Heidi was like Barbara. Not in looks – Barb was a skinny little sheep who made a virtue of being the smallest of us all – but in being argumentative, and in holding a grudge. Being difficult and bossy. But Barbara had at least not gone through life having superfluous babies by random men.

I slept badly that night. Something was niggling at me about that photo – the one of Pauline that they had at the February event. I had a copy of that as well and eventually I searched it out. There We were, as like as two peas, as Nan used to say, but I knew which was which. And I knew that the one in shorts, the one on the left, was me. They – whoever had done it, probably Alan, – had cut off Pauline and left me, displayed, impersonating her in public. It made me disorientated and dizzy, as if a mistake had been made about which of us had died.

Since I've been retired I've had no excuse not to go down there in February, but it's a sadly diminished event. This year Olive was ill and the whole thing was abandoned, or at least put off until the summer – that was before the rest of the year was cancelled for all of the population. But even in the years before that, without Eddie and Jim to kick it into motion, there were fewer and people who even knew what it was all about.

Only Alan and Barbara are left – and me. Maureen died quite suddenly and surprisingly, not long after her husband. Jim and Eddie made it to eighty-four and then died within weeks of each other, leaving Olive and Verona to move in together and struggle on. Barbara is still going, living independently, phoning me once a week to complain about Alison and how she hogs all the attention even though Alan and Barbara are more ill than she is.

These days I seem to go down there only for funerals – Eddie, Jim and Maureen so far – and I do it out of duty only, and I come home on the train feeling flat and tired, and full of the notion that I've missed something. As if there was an opportunity for something – I never know exactly what – and I've missed it. And it was nobody's fault but mine.

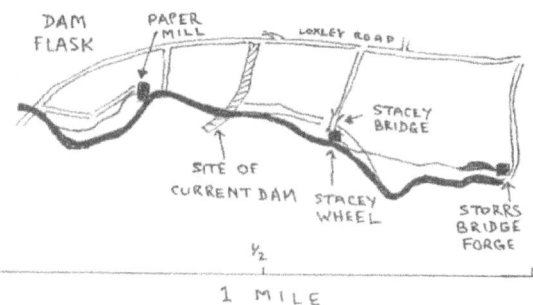
Through the rest of that half-term week the rain and sleet kept on coming. Heidi phoned and said she couldn't manage to do any more clearing of the bungalow. Jojo was off school and at home every day. He needed a walk daily but it was difficult for her because the baby had begun to crawl and was refusing to get into his pushchair or be constrained in any way.

'He's into everything,' she said. 'I can't take my eyes off him. Thank goodness Cassie's at nursery, she'd kill him if she saw him messing with her stuff.'

'What's Jarv doing?' I said. 'He could come over and help me empty the loft.'

It turned out, unsurprisingly, that Jarvis was kept busy helping his mother – taking Jojo out for his daily walk, which was a slow and boring job as he wanted to stop and look at every lamp-post, every tree and gate, and insisted – though not in words – that they go the same route very time.

I was pretty miserable myself. With no work to go to – though I had work to do – I languished. Another fine old-fashioned word. I got up late. I ate toast throughout the day, sometimes just with butter but often with chocolate spread as well. I smoked more than I really wanted to, just for something to do. I looked at the pile of stuff that needed sorting out and closed the door on it. I started drinking early in the evening and went to bed late and lay wakeful, bothering myself about questions like: Where were Pauline's ashes? And what would Heidi want to do with them? And would I have a say in it, would she let me? Even when I got to sleep I was restless and when I woke I felt no better for it. I lay in bed trying to go back to sleep and when I finally gave up and got up it was late morning.

I hated myself for all of this. I knew my sisters would tell me off if they could see me, not just Maureen and Barbara but *her* too. She. Pauline. 'Stop feeling sorry for yourself,' she would have said. 'There's plenty worse off than you.' Well, yes, but she was one of them wasn't she. Or maybe not. Maybe being dead would be an improvement; it often felt as if it would.

It seemed that the only thing I had that would allow me a little peace was Terry's flood project. He hadn't contacted me, and I appreciated that though it left me wondering if he had found someone else to take it on. But I found I didn't care if he had. I had some passing thoughts about the format, and the problems that might arise. There was the issue of how much detail to put in, both in terms of walk instructions and in terms of the history. There was the issue of the map – who could draw it, or was it all right to photocopy from the Ordnance Survey? There was a question in my mind about photographs, but I thought probably the budget wouldn't run as far as that.

But I felt no need to solve any possible problems. I just had an odd feeling that walking by the river, and thinking about all those people, swept from their beds and carried away and drowned, gave me some respite from thinking about her, my sister. Perspective even, maybe, one day, I hoped. Prospective perspective. And so I started out on the next bit of the journey.

I knew it would come to this sooner or later. I had been putting off this next bit of the trail in spite of the way it was nagging at me, and the reason, I knew full well, was that We occasionally used to walk her dog this way. Rare occasions, maybe once or twice only, when I could persuade her to ferret out a pair of trainers and risk being seen in public in her gardening trousers, maybe only two or three occasions over the last ten years, say, but enough that I did not know if I would be able to do it.

However. Saturday. I was pleased it was a day of strong wind and sudden sharp showers. I would never have been able to persuade her to go out into the country on a day like that. And I walked the opposite way from my usual one, by starting at Low Bradfield and going round clockwise. At first it was hard to concentrate on what I was doing. Images of her belongings in black binbags crowded into my mind and drove out what I should have been thinking about. I had to look hard at the water and try to imagine it as river, stream even, not a lake, and then as a roaring wall of water barrelling down through the dark.

"The Dale Dyke, just below Bradfield joins the Agden Brook and together they become the Loxley River and now flow into Damflask reservoir. Underneath the waters lies the old hamlet of Damflask, where three men and a boy were drowned in a wire mill, while working through the night."

This was another good story for Year Ten students. That a boy, and he was not the only one of their own age and younger, was working, *at night*, in a wire mill which I explained, though I never actually looked up the process of wire making, was a small factory making the wire hoops that made the framework for crinoline dresses, was both fascinating to them, and horrifying. They would ask how much he would earn, (maybe a shilling a day, though of course they wouldn't know what a shilling was either) and why his parents allowed him to go to work. They asked what his name was – it was John Ibbotson – Ibbotsons were all over the story of the flood and my pupils would know there were still Ibbotsons in Sheffield; I had taught quite a few. The boys claimed that they would have jumped out of an upstairs window and run away, uphill from the flood waters.

Light relief, after that, was the story of the sensible miller who carried all his sacks of corn and flour to the upstairs rooms of his mill, and then went home to take his wife, and his horse and cows to a safe place. All his lifting and carrying were in vain however because his entire mill was washed away, along with his pig. For some reason, the kids liked stories with pigs in them, though the information that an ordinary family would keep a pig in their backyard tended to baffle them.

In spite of the wind and wet I seemed to feel slightly better once I was walking under the lively clouds, looking out for signs of green in the hedge bottoms and on the hawthorns. Only one sailing dinghy was out on the water, tacking against the wind, but there were several fisherman hunched along the bank. None of them spoke to me, but then, I didn't speak to them.

As far as this bit of the trail went, there was nothing to see. All gone, bridge, houses, mills, boys and men, washed away by the gathering speed of the flood waters, and then, years later, dammed and flooded to make another reservoir for the growing city.

At the halfway point, at the dam end of the reservoir, I glanced over the wall and remembered, without wishing to, the time We had looked over the same wall and noticed some unusual ducks. She saw them first.

'What are those?' she said.

They had green patches over their eyes, like a design stencilled on and outlined in gold. 'Just ducks,' I said.

'What sort of ducks?' she said. 'Even I can tell you they're not the same as park ducks.'

I didn't want to but I had to admit that I didn't know. 'I'll look them up when we get home.'

They were teal, it turned out, not that uncommon but something I had not seen before.

'See,' she said, sitting in my front room, drinking tea, 'if it wasn't for me you wouldn't have looked at them properly and We would never have known what they were. It's a good job I was with you.'

And she was no longer with me. Neither were there any teal there, only a couple of mallards, and I was not sure whether to be glad or sorry.

It did me no real harm, that walk. I would not admit it to Maureen, but getting out in the fresh air, in the wet cold fresh air seemed to give me something else to be miserable about, so that when I got home I had a hot shower and put on my pyjamas and Pauline's dressing gown and made myself a meal of oven chips and a piece of battered fish from the freezer. Then I laid out all my school tasks on the dining table (which I never used for dining) and arranged them in order of urgency, and held off the whisky all evening. Next day was Sunday, last day of the half-term holiday, and I got through the tasks, still in nightwear, as the rain bashed on the windows and the wind rattled the letterbox in the front door so that several times I got up to see if it was Jarvis coming to visit. But it never was.

But I finished the work. I even went through my cupboards and the freezer and made a list, mostly of quite reasonably nourishing items, that I needed to buy. Before I went to bed I finished up the loaf, toasted, with chocolate spread and used up the end of a tub of ice cream, so that I had more room in the freezer.

Back at school on Monday morning I felt a small comfort in being in my familiar place, and also, when the kids started trickling into the form room, a small nip of pleasure to see that Daisy was amongst them, on time. I decided not to say anything to her but to leave well alone – she was talking with girls she'd been friends with all through school, she looked less well-groomed than the norm for their set, but animated enough and – important sign – she was carrying a school bag. I did not ask her for a note from her mother explaining her previous absences, I did not even ask her for her History homework, I did not even smile at her, but I gave her a small nod of acknowledgement and appreciation that I had clocked that she was there.

Josh and Kane, who always moved as one, were not present but I saw them later, sauntering through the gates in time for morning break, and I used up my own precious morning break in calling their mothers to come in to school to discuss what we should have discussed at Consultation Evening.

I knew Kane's mother. She was called Kerry and I had taught her – not much – back in the 1980s. She and Josh's mother were somehow related; one of them's aunt was the other one's grandmother or some such ramification, and they lived on the same street. I invited them to come together, since I knew that they would anyway, being as inseparable as their respective sons were.

'I do try,' said Kerry. She was rocking a pushchair with a baby in it; not one of hers, she explained but she was looking after it as a favour.

'She does try,' said Josh's mother. She was pale and weedy like her son, while Kerry was comfortably round – you could say fat. The two boys sat close together, trying not to look shifty.

'I'm sure,' I said, without conviction. 'Look,' I said, 'we're nearly there. A few more weeks and they'll be sitting their exams. No one's expecting them to get A-stars, but they'll get something if they come to the revision sessions and come for the exams. That's all we're asking.'

'Kane doesn't like exams,' said Kerry. 'He gets nervous.'

'So does Josh.'

'I'm not expecting them to *like* it,' I said. 'I'm just – school's just – expecting them to get on and *do* it. Like all the other kids.'

'I never got any exams,' said Josh's mum.

'I got some,' said Kerry. 'But it never did me any good.' The baby started fussing and she rocked it more vigorously.

'We're duggies,' said Kane. 'There's no point, we're always in duggie groups, we don't learn anything.'

I knew there was no point arguing with this. No amount of telling them how capable they could be if they put their minds to it would change the conviction that they were stupid, especially as the conviction gave them a handy excuse for not even – ever – taking the risk of trying.

'Look at it this way,' I said, passing the exam timetables across the desk, 'Maths, English, Science, those are the main ones. Art, they don't mind doing that do they? Technology – just need to finish off their coursework, as far as I know. It's February now. March, April, they need to come into school every day. May – revision sessions – they need to be there, but it's not all day every day. End of May, through June, an exam here and there, then they're free to leave and get a job or go to college.'

Both women laughed. 'College!'

'Another thing,' I said. 'You know don't you, they can only go to the prom if they have attended school. I'm talking ninety seven percent, no late marks.' I was making this up. 'That's confidential,' I added. 'You're the first people I've told. New rule.'

They looked at each other. 'OK,' said Kerry.

When they had gone – it had taken nearly all of my free period – I thought about Kerry. She hadn't been in my form but I had taught her for several of her years in school. She might even have taken an Integrated Humanities GCSE; maybe that was one of the exams that she got but which never did her any good. There'd been nothing memorable about her, not especially rowdy, not especially stubborn or lazy, just a girl getting through the days and waiting till she could leave and start her proper life. And look where that got her. Into a similar boat to the one Heidi was in, though Heidi had a better grip on her children and never looked or sounded as defeated, at least not until her mother died.

It was March. The evenings were beginning to lengthen out and there was no more getting up in the dark. I was working through the papers I'd taken from the bungalow, dealing with insurance companies and building societies, now that probate had finally come through.

There was no money. It should not have been a surprise to me, and it wasn't, really, although I had not been quite up to date with her credit card debt. She spent it, you see, she gave money to Heidi and presents to the children all the time, she added to her mortgage when she felt like it. She had not – ever – let me know that she was living above her income; I would have done something about it if she had. But a dinner out with friends now and again on a Saturday did not account for an overdraft this size, and I blamed Heidi.

Heidi managing on benefits, plus some attendance allowance for Jojo, and whatever her current bloke would chip in. Heidi having more babies than was strictly necessary and being unable to go out to work, beyond a little unofficial child-minding for neighbours, and a sideline on e-bay. I let her know that there would not be any great bequest coming her way from the estate and she shrugged as if she had not expected it.

'There's still the bungalow,' she said.

'You won't get it all,' I said. 'There's solicitors and estate agents to pay.'

'I know that,' she said. 'It's not for me anyway, I'll put it in the bank for Jojo, so that he has it in the future, to look after him.' I knew she meant it when she said it; I also knew that there would come a time when she would have to break into 'Jojo's money' to get through some emergency, and she would never be able to pay it back. She operated no more in the real world than her mother had, when it came to money.

Then there was Gavin deciding we should sue the department store where it happened.

'Criminal negligence,' he said, unattractively eager.

'How?' I said. 'Tell me what they did that they should not have done, or did not do that they should have done.'

'They must have done something wrong,' he said. 'They should be made to pay.'

'For what?' I said.

And he ranted on and said he was going to a solicitor, and even Heidi told him it was pointless, and I just felt helplessly angry that he was making us all feel worse than we already did.

'It was an accident,' I said. I shouted actually, and made the baby cry. 'What is it about the word 'accident' that you don't get? She tripped. There was an inquest, remember. Did they say it was anybody's fault? No.'

'No harm in asking a solicitor,' he said.

'You are only interested in getting some money out of all this,' I said. 'I find you a deeply loathsome human being.'

I got up and got my coat. By the time I was at the front door Jarvis was beside me.

'Shall I see you home?' he said. He had never offered that before and I was touched, even though I thought it was a ludicrous suggestion. Heidi came out into the hall too.

'He won't do it,' she said. 'Even if he does I won't let it go any further.' She sighed and I had the hope that maybe Gavin really would soon be on his way, as all Heidi's men were before long.

The bungalow was emptied except for the furniture, and tidied and cleaned and on the market, and one evening after school I went there to see how the garden was doing.

We were not brought up to gardening. Our nan liked flowers but only had a small concreted back yard. She grew stocks and marigolds in pots, perched on the wall to catch the sun; she watered them every evening through the spring and summer. Auntie Vi didn't have time to set anything growing; there was a tiny patch of lawn and a lilac bush – lovely for a fortnight and dull for the rest of the year.

And We had different ideas about having a garden. For me, though it sounds dramatic to say it, it was a reason for living. It was peace and nourishment and employment. It was, I suppose, like a child; I could go to work and not think about it but it would be all the time there, under the surface, ready for me to come back to and think about if I had a spare moment; but when I was there, in it, present, it filled me with joy to see things growing and spreading and just *being*. For her it was one of the things a respectable person should have, like curtains or a refrigerator, and she was willing to spend a little time on it and a little money buying some pansies for the winter or a new rose but it was not part of the bedrock of her life. We had many enjoyable arguments about our gardens. She said my garden was untidy, that half my plants were weeds, that I didn't keep on top of it, as if it was an opponent of some kind, that I kept things long after they were past their best. I said she relied too much on seasonal bedding, that she pruned too hard and too early, that colourful didn't have to mean garish and that French marigolds were unpleasant flowers. We enjoyed those discussions and there was no one else I could have them with.

I went in through the side gate and looked at it. She had a tiny patch of lawn with a birdbath placed centrally, which to my mind looked ridiculous. I recalled the fuss there was about getting that damn birdbath in the right place – left a bit, right a bit – and Heidi's bloke as was then, who was doing the manhandling was probably urged to leave Heidi and his daughter by the process. The Bluestones at Stonehenge must have been aligned with less fuss.

The grass hadn't yet been cut by the man who came to do it – too wet – and it was looking green but shaggy. Personally, I never wished to have a lawn – waste of space, too much trouble, only use is for sitting on, which I don't do. There were crocuses out in the borders and the daffodil buds had turned themselves over and were ready to come out, just as soon as the rain stopped. It was going to be a late spring that year.

I thought while I was there I would just check inside. Sometimes people viewing the house would leave wardrobes open or dirty footprints on the floor – not something I would have worried too much about, but I knew *she* would have. So I went in through the kitchen door.

At first I thought she had been broken into and burgled. There were tools on the worktop and dust and plaster, and something was missing. It was the glass-fronted wall cabinet which she used to display some pretty bits of china – fancy teapots and such, not to my taste at all; the cabinet was gone and there were rough holes where it had been fixed on the wall.

It was a shock. Worse than that, it was a violation as if someone was stamping on her grave – if she'd had one that is, instead of being ash in a jar, tidily labelled in some back room at the undertakers. I stayed calm but inside I was gasping for breath and wishing I had not opened the door. I took out my phone and called Heidi.

She answered straight away. 'Hello Pam.' She sounded tired.

'Heidi,' I said, 'I don't want to alarm you but there's a bit of damage in your mum's kitchen. Do you –?'

'What are you doing there?'

'Just watering the plants. Someone's been here and taken a cupboard off the wall –'

'I know,' she said, and now she sounded close to tears. 'Don't worry, I know all about it. He's going to clear up the mess.'

So it was, as I had half-known, Gavin.

'What did he think he was playing at?'

'Don't start Pam, all right. He'll sort it. At the weekend.'

I shouldn't have given her a hard time but I couldn't stop myself. 'How could you do that Heidi? Why did you let him do that?'

'What of it?' she said wearily. 'You never liked it.'

'You could have asked me.'

'I don't have to ask your permission to do anything,' she said. 'The bungalow is mine. The contents are mine.'

'So why do you want that cabinet? It won't fit in your kitchen. You hate that pretty-pretty china. It's made a proper mess of the wall – you can't sell it with that sort of mess all over. And why didn't you tell me? I'm really angry Heidi, I don't need this.'

'You think I do?' she said.

'So where is it?'

'At his mum's. She wanted it. I didn't want it. She's got it. OK?'

I detected the hours of arguing there had been before she was tired enough to give in. 'What about her china? Has she got that too?'

'Look, don't you start giving me a hard time. Gavin wanted it for his Mum.'

'And you let him? You think that makes it any better? You should have said no.'

'I said no,' she said. She sounded so tired and down I almost wanted to let her off.

'I said no,' she said again. 'I don't know how many times I said no.'

'It's your house,' I said. 'He has no right –'

'I know,' she said. 'It's mine, not yours. And you have no right. Mine. I can go and burn it down if I feel like it. And right now,' she said loudly, the tiredness gone from her, 'I do feel like it.'

And she shut off her phone and did not answer when I rang again.

Jarvis was sitting on my front wall again. This time, however, his pale face was looking more cheerful.

I shifted a few newspapers and CDs to make space for his mug on the table.

'What is it then?'

'What do you mean?'

'Come on Jarv. I know you. What is making you grin like a Cheshire cat?'

'Why do people say that? About a Cheshire cat? It doesn't make sense.'

'Probably not, if you haven't read Alice in Wonderland.'

'It's a book for little kids isn't it?'

'Never mind. Come on, tell me.'

'Gavin's gone.'

I thought I should think carefully before I said anything, though I couldn't stop a bit of a smile myself.

'Gone for good?'

He obviously hadn't thought of this. 'I think so. He's took all his stuff anyway. Gone back to live at his mum's.'

'And how is your mum?' Though I could make a good guess. It would have been Heidi who called a halt to a relationship, suddenly and without mercy. Gavin had been getting above himself and meddling in family matters that didn't concern him – that would be what had brought things towards a close. The business with the china cabinet would have just about put the tin lid on it, as Auntie Vi used to say.

'She's OK I think,' said Jarvis.

'A good thing,' I said, 'is that the baby isn't his. You wouldn't want him coming round for visits.'

'And Cassie isn't his,' said Jarvis joyfully. 'And I'm not his, and Jojo's not his. So we never have to see *him.*'

We both, I think, remembered at that instant that Jarvis did have to see *his* father, his and Jojo's, though less and less often these days. I asked him. 'Seen Alasdair lately?'

'Easter holidays,' he said. Some of the light went out of his face. 'But only one weekend. And anyway, he's in Skegness now. It's OK.'

The father of Jojo and Jarvis was called Alasdair. He was four or five years older than Heidi, a tall, suave young man from the leafy end of the city. His mother was a psychiatrist, his father some sort of academic and what they thought of Heidi We were never to find out because he seemed to have no communication with them and We were never introduced. Alasdair I found shallow and boastful; Pauline said he needed a direction in life and something to focus him on the usefulness of a job. Whether she thought that Heidi would provide that direction – well, she did think that, it was obvious. She believed the best of Alasdair, as she believed the best of lots of people, and it was wasted on him.

We sat in a companionable sort of way in my kitchen and got through some tea and biscuits.

'You know,' said Jarvis, 'I could help you in your garden.'

'What would you do?'

'I can weed. I can dig. I can tidy up.'

'Do you do it at home?' I knew he didn't. Heidi's back yard was an eyesore littered with bikes and balls and broken things.

'I used to help Trev. He showed me how to do stuff. I can cut the grass.'

'I don't have much grass, only the paths. Anyway, who's Trev?'

'Granma's friend. He does stuff in her garden. Used to.'

'I thought her gardener was called Barry.'

'I know him too,' said Jarvis. 'But he only cuts the hedge and the grass and washes the patio. Got a pressure washer, see.'

'So she had two gardeners?'

'Not really,' he said. 'Trev likes gardening but he lives in a flat. He got divorced, see. So he did gardening at Granma's and she cooked him a nice meal. Not every weekend, just now and again.'

'Oh,' I said.

'And I thought,' he said, 'when Mum doesn't need me, now Gavin's gone she says she's going to be more sort of – there for us kids, and I kind of like doing the garden and I could come and help you.'

'We'll see,' I said. I was not keen to open any dialogue with Heidi. 'Anyway, thank you for coming to tell me. About Gavin. Did your Mum ask you to?'

'She doesn't know I came,' he said. 'But I thought – I just thought –'

'You thought I'd like to know,' I said in my best 'understanding' manner.

'I thought you might come and see us again if you knew Gavin wasn't there.'

Did he think I was scared of Gavin? 'I'm not scared of Gavin, if that's what you all think.'

'No,' he said. 'I just thought Mum would like to see you.'

Oh no she wouldn't. 'Where do you get that idea from?' I said.

'She's on her own,' he said.

For now, I thought.

'When Granma – she used to come and see us.'

I got the idea. Whatever she told Jarvis Heidi needed some childcare, now that her mum wasn't there to step in almost on a daily basis, and now that Gavin was gone.

'We miss her,' he said, getting a bit tearful.

'I'm sure you do,' I said. 'But I don't think I'd be a substitute. It's not like a football match you know.'

'You're our Auntie,' he said. 'It's better than nothing.'

'Thank you for being honest,' I said. It came out sarcastically, as it was meant to do.

Fathers. Our experience of them was sketchy. Our own dad I could believe to have been a good enough one, at least when he had our mum to share the job with. He was a short, heavy man, always with dark stubble on his chin, though he shaved every day with a razor that hung inside the back door with its leather strap for sharpening. Most of the time he was at work, or else at his house a mile or so away from us. 'He's got his own life to live,' our nan said to us when we complained, but the words didn't mean much to us. Later We wondered if she meant that he had a lady friend, but if he did We never knew about her.

He was always nice to us, with sixpences and lollipops when We were small, and money for the pictures or the swimming pool when We were bigger. He was pleased and proud when We went off to college and though by then he was living on his pension he used to put a pound note in the letters he sometimes sent to us, and once, a cheque for twenty pounds, two cheques, one each. Maybe that was our share of the pools win.

When We were thirteen We moved in with Auntie Vi, partly because Nan was finding it harder work, and partly because Auntie Vi's husband had died and she wanted some company. Alan by then was out at work, and he stayed with Nan and contributed a third of his wages – one pound five shillings – every week for his keep.

Auntie Vi was what Nan called 'a strapping big woman.' She wore severe suits with brooches on the lapel and had a shampoo and set every Friday after work. She was our mum's younger sister, so much younger than our nan, and with different expectations. We were at first shocked and affronted at the differences and clamoured to go back, but We had to get over it. Our nan was a laid-back, comfortable sort of person, always ready to put off cooking a meal, say, and sending us for chips instead. Auntie Vi had routines and made it clear to us what she expected. Our dirty clothes were never to be left on the floor but put in a special wicker basket in the bathroom, and only then would she add them to the weekly wash in the twin-tub. We were to change our beds every Saturday, without being told, and put the old sheets in a different basket on the landing. We were to be in for our tea every evening, unless We gave notice in advance. We could go out Friday evenings till nine, and Saturdays till half past, unless We were going to the pictures, which made us home later, and then she had to know what We were going to see, and who with and We had to recount the plot to her afterwards. She managed to change our school to the grammar school, how I don't know, unless she played the orphans-of-the-flood card. She checked our homework and made us get a good night's sleep. She was doing it all for our own good,

We knew that, and she told us that it was how our own mum would have brought us up if she was still alive.

She told us the facts of life, or her version of them at least. Basically – 'Keep your knees together and don't forget what happened to Maureen and Barbara.'

'But it's a good thing in a way,' said Pauline, when our periods started shortly after we got there. 'I can't see Nan dealing with this, can you?'

'She's probably forgotten it ever happened to her,' I said. 'And at least we've got an indoor toilet now.'

Pauline learned a lot from Vi. She really took to seeing how cooking was done, and cleaning, and managing. She was given the job of doing the ironing and she seemed to even like it, especially Vi's brisk little cotton shirts that she wore for work in the Co-op offices. I suppose I was more like Nan, slatternly and easy going about dirt and food and what people might think.

A few years later, when We had both qualified as teachers – in other words, had gone as far up the professional status ladder as anyone in the family had ever dreamed of – and Auntie Vi and our dad had come to see us receive our certificates, and We had seen them off on the bus back down south, and were walking back through town, Pauline said to me, 'Pam, I've got something to tell you.'

I was surprised, for what could she have to tell me that I didn't already know, and I never lost that moment of surprise. She was pregnant, that was what she had to tell me, and the surprise was not that she had a boyfriend – she had many and I believed I knew about all of them – but that she should be pregnant, and I didn't know about it – that didn't seem possible. Something like that – I should have known without her having to tell me, I should have been able to *feel* it. I knew that I was being weird, and I didn't say anything, but it was a real feeling – I still have it when I think of the whole process We went through to have Heidi. How could she do this thing without me? How could she change so, her body and her weight and even her hair and face changed, and mine didn't and this had never happened before.

The thought that she was going to give birth to an actual baby – that idea I think I must have put out of my head completely. I wouldn't look at it. Just, every time she came into a room, looking – wrong – I had to wrench my brain into remembering what was happening.

Of course it played havoc with our plans. We had moved together into a nicer and more expensive flat and started our first teaching jobs – in different schools from each other – only two months before. The boyfriend had departed, probably en route to India if he could find his way there, unaware of what he had set in motion. The baby that was going to be Heidi was expected in May.

'I don't want him to know,' she said. 'He won't have anything to offer. It wasn't a big love affair or anything.'

'Then why did you do it?' I said.

She looked at me, only looked and I knew what she meant. She meant, Who are you to talk? You've done it as well, haven't you. She was right, I had, though I hadn't enjoyed it.

'Ever heard of contraception?' I said.

'I know,' she said. 'I came off the pill didn't I, when I split up with John, – you remember John – and – I don't know – it all happened and I thought I would get away with it. I'm sorry Pammy.'

She didn't seem to be as sorry as I was. Seemed to be quite pleased in a wry sort of way, I thought.

'You'll lose your job,' I said.

'What I thought,' she said, 'was that I could work till Easter. They can't sack me if I'm turning up for work. Then I'll claim some benefits. People have babies all the time you know, without having a job. They can't let us starve. Then, when he's a bit older and I can leave him with you, I can get some sort of job in the evenings – bar work, or something. We can manage.'

We did manage. We managed pretty well, I would say, for the first few years.

She did better than bar work; she taught evening classes, which still existed in numbers at that time. Two or three evenings a week I would come home from work and it would be my job to put Heidi to bed, completely on my own – bath, bottle, story, sing a song, bed. I was just as good at it as her mother was, I was just as attentive to her needs, just as excited when she started to walk and talk and become even more her own little person.

I was very fond of her when she was little. She was a cheery, determined little girl, quite independent in practical ways – dressing herself, and getting on with little projects without a lot of bothering of adults. She liked school, she had plenty of friends, she didn't mind, as a young child, when her mother had a boyfriend, or another, different boyfriend, or one that moved in with them. *I* minded – that was when I moved out and bought my own place. Not far away though, and I still saw a lot of Heidi. She used to say she had two mothers, and when she was small that felt fine, as if two mothers would make up for not having a father. If anyone had told us what a problem that would turn into by the time she reached her teens We might have behaved differently. I say 'We.' I always say 'We.'

Heidi always looked older than she was, and she had an air of purpose about her, right from the start, so that even at playgroup she was allowed to choose for herself what she played with, and with whom. She had the air of someone who *would* choose for herself, whether anyone else liked it or not. She was supremely confident and self-reliant and We were proud of her for it.

She never looked like us. I can only surmise that she looked like whoever her father was. As a child she had brown hair, as shiny as a new conker, and light brown eyes. Her hair is darker now, but still shiny and well cared for, an altogether different substance from what the rest of the Dearly family has on its heads. She is tall too, long and skinny when she was young, now heavier, and more impressive.

Trouble started, as it usually does, when she was a teenager. She looked older than she was. She hung around with girls who were older than she was. She pushed against the rules, she argued and sulked and flounced – all of this We knew was normal, We were teachers weren't We – but there was not, in Heidi, the smallest notion that it could ever – *ever* – be her that should be the one to give in. Stubborn didn't begin to describe it. Obdurate, hard, unyielding. And unfortunately, given to making bad decisions from which she then could not extract herself. I wasn't living with them at that time, but I still saw enough of her to know that she was what they called 'troubled.' Awkward is another word. Cussed. A pain in the backside. A little cow.

We managed between us to keep her in school until Year 10, though at the cost of many meetings with the Head of Year, the Education Welfare Officer and some sort of counsellor, and many calls from the school – not, thank goodness, either of the schools where We were teaching – telling us that she had gone missing again, been excluded for smoking, got into a fight with another girl. Et cetera. At the bottom of it, as far as I could see, was the idea she had that somewhere her father – 'her real father' as she said – was wondering about her and just waiting for a chance to take her away and treat her properly. No matter how Pauline explained that she had only ever known him by the name of Bonesy and had never known where he lived or where he came from, no matter how often I told Heidi that she was lucky to have a good mother and other people who cared about her – no matter what sense was talked to her she persisted. Probably – I've never asked her – she had a magical belief that if she behaved badly enough her mother would give way and miraculously turn up Bonesy out of several billion men on the planet. There were times when I thought Pauline would have been pleased to do so, *and* let him take her off our hands.

Heidi had an abortion when she was sixteen. Yes I know the word termination doesn't sound quite as brutal, but I prefer to call it like it is. And went straight back out and got pregnant again. That's not entirely true – that she got pregnant again immediately. No, she waited till she had struggled – we all three struggled – halfway through the sixth form and *then* she went and got pregnant again. Jojo was born on the day she should have been sitting her first A level. Pauline was quite relaxed about it. 'I never expected her to pass anyway,' she said.

I couldn't say whether or not I felt as much for her as her actual mother did. Probably not. Certainly I felt more than I did for any of the other nieces and nephews, but that could be explained just by how much time I spent with her, how well I knew her, how much she had once upon a time relied on me. And what measure would her mother and I use to decide how deeply fond we each felt? There are only ridiculous lines from ridiculously soppy songs to describe love.

'Whatever was she thinking of?' I said. This was when Jarvis was about eleven and Jojo was twelve, and Heidi's life had seemed to me to be on an even keel.

'I don't know that *thinking* comes into it,' said Pauline, excusing herself once again as well as Heidi.

'Don't give me that,' I said. 'She should have been prepared, *before* the thinking went out of the window. How is she going to manage, with Jojo the way he is? He's a full time job in himself, without adding another problem.'

'You would,' said Pauline, 'call a little baby a problem. What do you know about it anyway? It's not as if she's a teenager now, is it.'

There was plenty I could have said at that point but I held it in.

I woke with a sore throat. These used to be worse in the days of chalk dust, now can only be put down to overuse of the voice and the multitudes of germs that people generate. I took two paracetamol and went to school; by ten o'clock the effect had worn off and I now had a sore head as well.

'Go home,' said Caroline, the headteacher, to me, when she found me cadging more paracetamol off the office staff. 'You look awful.'

'I'll be all right,' I said.

'Go home,' said Frank Midgely. He came into my classroom especially to tell me. 'You'll only make yourself worse, trying to tough it out.'

'I'll be all right,' I said.

'For fuck's sake,' said Angie Willis the French teacher in the staff room at dinner time. 'Don't give me your beastly cold. Go home. Take your nasty germs away. I've only just got over the last one.' A self-centred woman, Angie.

I got through the afternoon and left school on the dot of three-forty-five, as soon as the kids did. Caroline saw me going. 'Stay at home tomorrow,' she said. 'If I see you in here I'll march you off home myself. Understand?'

I pretended I hadn't heard her.

Maureen phoned that evening – I could imagine that Verona had written out a schedule and given a copy to each person in the family, highlighted where their turn was.

I sneezed into the phone, which set me off coughing.

'You don't sound good,' said Maureen.

'I'll be all right,' I said. 'Just a bit of a cold.'

'Are you looking after yourself?'

'Of course I am,' I said, truthfully because I had a glass of whisky by my side. If I was to have a day off school tomorrow I was entitled to a drink tonight.

'And how's Heidi doing,' she said.

'She's fine,' I said, from a position of complete ignorance.

'I wish I could come up and see you all,' she said.

I coughed rather a lot to give myself time to think of an answer. Then I said, 'Mm.'

I had a day off school, during which I was completely miserable. I spoke to no one and did nothing. I watched daytime television and fell asleep on the settee in an unnatural position which gave me a stiff neck. I heated up a tin of soup and rooted through the freezer until I found half a tub of ice cream which got me through the evening along with several mugs of hot chocolate. I laid off the whisky, partly because I was determined to go into school the next day even if I had come out in pustules and partly because there was none left.

And I did go, dosed and equipped with paracetamol, and I made it through and it was not too bad. And in the evening Maureen called to say that she and Barbara were inviting themselves up for a visit during my Easter holiday. They were coming on the train and would I meet them at the station because they would have Easter eggs for the children and didn't want them being squashed on the bus. They must have nothing better to do, I thought, than to cart a ton of overpriced chocolate from one end of the country to the other.

They had never stayed with me before, only with Pauline, and it meant I would not only have to plan and cook actual meals but also that I must tackle the spare bedroom, where lay, on the beds and on the floor, in bags and boxes, all the things I had taken from the bungalow, some with Heidi's knowledge and permission, some without.

I started with the clothes. We were the same size, Pauline and me, but not since – well, maybe not since We were schoolgirls – had anyone been *un*able to tell us apart from the way we dressed. When We were young it was an everyday occurrence, that people, even Nan, did not know who was who. Not that We wore matching clothes but back then We didn't have our own clothes either; Nan just put a pile of clothes on the chair in our bedroom and We got out of bed and put them on. We went to school dressed any-old-how and no one knew which of us was which.

As I said, our family name was Dearly. The first time I – We – became aware of it was when they made us sing, in infants school, There is a Green Hill Far Away. Why I wonder, was it considered suitable for a class of five year olds to be singing about dying and blood and suffering? But maybe it did us no harm. What it did do was produce a whole playtime of children prancing round us, me and my sister, chorusing 'oh dearly, dearly.' As if it was funny. I suppose it was. I was inclined to be upset and made fists of my hands but my sister said 'It's all right. They ain't going to hurt us' and they didn't. After that We were often called the Dearly Dearlies, even by our teacher, and it didn't hurt us at all but made us even a bit more special than We already were. There were any number of things that made us special. Having no mother, and being twins, and not only twins and not only identical, but having different birthdays, and middle names that reminded us of it, she being born just before midnight on the 30ᵗʰ of June, me born just after midnight on the first of July. Pauline June Dearly and Pamela July Dearly, our mother had named us, whether as a way of remembering which of us was the elder, or for some less functional reason We never had the chance to ask her about. There were times when I was young that my brother Alan could make me cry by telling me that Pauline was a month older than me. It was always easy to make me cry.

When we eventually went to a school with uniform no one had a hope of telling us apart, neither teachers nor the other girls. The school put us into separate classes – that was probably for some administrative or practical reason but I believed it was because they knew I was cleverer than she was. Actually, in a way, that was true; I was cleverer than she was, at maths and English and remembering things and working things out. She had better practical skills and was better at making friends, but that was all right. I didn't need friends so much if I had my sister. My sister who looked exactly the same as I did.

Later, we diverged. She went in more for dresses and wearing shoes that matched her handbag; I wore cord Levi's and a jacket from the Army and Navy Stores. I kept my hair short – which is, as I told her, much the best thing to do with rough crinkly hair like ours – but she tried and tried to turn hers into something smooth and shining. And long, which really was a lost cause before she started. And you can make it blond or black or auburn, but frizzy hair is still frizzy hair. I think over the years her hair caused her more grief than Heidi did.

Anyway, here in the back bedroom were all her clothes, bundled into black bin bags in a way that would have riled her just a bit and piled on the twin beds where Maureen and Barbara were going to have to sleep. I was not going to hang them in my wardrobe – the last thing I could have coped with was to experience the shock of finding her in there some future dark morning. Some of the clothes were ordinary and charity-shoppable – but they were the very things, ordinary M & S jumpers and trousers, that I could keep and wear without feeling like an imposter. *Could* I, I wondered, actually wear these plain jumpers, in unobjectionable colours? And if I did, would it make me happier or more miserable? Would I get used to it? Would someone at work notice and confront me with the question – Is that Pauline's jumper you're wearing? Would I ever forget that it had once been hers? I could not work it out but I did at least decide to put all of that sort of thing, the unremarkable sort of thing, in one pile, and move on to the more difficult stuff.

She had clothes for Occasions. I didn't know what all these Occasions can have been – the only thing I ever went to that needed a bit of dressing up was the annual Year 11 prom, where if I turned up in my ordinary school trouser suit the kids got a bit insulted and accused me of disrespecting their big night. Pauline though had a social life. She was invited out for meals with groups of people – all those strangers who descended on her funeral I suppose – and they would have outings to the races or to flower shows or to go round Chatsworth or Harewood House. She went to things at the Lyceum, with dinner before or after. So she had dresses, and jackets to go with them, she had garments of floaty stuff and sparkly stuff and when I looked at the labels even I knew that they had taken quite a bit out of her wages. She had several coats for different sorts of outings, a whole bag full of scarves, every colour you could imagine, now tipped and piled on the bed like a soft kind of treasure. Handbags of various colours and shapes and sizes.

'You should try something a bit brighter,' she said to me, more than once.

'I do it the easy way,' I said. 'I don't want to be getting up in the morning and wondering what to wear.'

'But it doesn't have to be all grey,' she said.

'It's not,' I said.

'No it's not,' she said. 'You've got black and navy as well. And why trouser suits? They went out decades ago.'

'Practical,' I said. 'Will you shut up now. What I look like is my business.'

'Fine,' she said. 'If you want the kids to say you're a lesbian.'

'Do they?' I said. I was not surprised. 'Well, maybe I am.' And We both laughed.

I picked up a scarf from the heap and put it near my face. I could smell perfume though I couldn't say what it was called. Scent is supposed to be evocative but I couldn't say that it did any evoking to me.

I sat on a chair and looked at the heaps of clothes. They were too good to throw out, too good for a charity shop. I knew there were shops that would take clothes – designer stuff – and sell it for a commission, but I would feel a fraud going in one. What if someone looked at me in my old duffel coat and knew I had stolen someone else's wardrobe? Worse, if they thought they were mine? I went downstairs to make a cup of tea and wondered what Heidi would want to do with them. Would it upset her too much to sell them? Should I invite her to come over and help me sort out which should go where? But I remembered she wasn't speaking to me.

In the end I got my suitcases down from the top of the wardrobe and shook the clothes and folded them carefully and put them gently in as if I was laying babies in their beds. If – *if* –Maureen and Barbara were in a pleasant frame of mind, I would ask their advice. There might be things there that they would take off my hands, they might take something – scarves maybe – for Verona and Olive. One of the beds at least was ready to be made up and slept in.

I made room in a downstairs cupboard, high in the kitchen, for all the things that had been passed down to us from Nan and from Auntie Vi. There was nothing of value, nothing even attractive, nothing that in my right mind I would have wanted to keep, and that was why it was Pauline who had kept them, rather than let me throw them out. Now though I did not know what to do with them. In all the years I had lived on my own I had managed to keep my home free of unnecessary ornaments. I was not going to have china flower baskets or a brass owl or a plate depicting a pirate ship on display. I did not want to set up anything like a shrine, even if no one else would see it that way. I did not want objects, even if they had been worth looking at, on view to remind me. There was already sufficient for that. I closed the door of the top cupboard with the satisfaction of knowing that I'd not abandoned anything to someone else's worthy cause and at the same time there was nothing in my sightline to make me remember when I didn't want to.

I went back upstairs to deal with the shoes. Obviously, they would all fit me. Just as obviously there were very few that I could actually wear. I could hear her saying, 'Go on Pam, a nice pair of shoes makes all the difference.' I took them all out and lined them up on the floor, in pairs. The very pairness of them made me want to spit. It crossed my mind to throw away just one of each pair and see how they liked it but I did not want to think I was insane and pushed the thought away. I kept her slippers, which were nicer than mine, and a pair of sandals and put the rest back in the bag. I thought I would let Barbara pick out any she might like to have – not Maureen, because she had bunions and wouldn't fit into any of them. It would be a sort of re-run of Cinderella.

That left a random collection of curtains and sheets and household goods that I did not know I had brought away. I put them all in the under-bed drawers until I should have some reason for looking in there. Maybe they would stay there, I thought, until the day when Heidi is clearing my house after I die. I hoped it would be Heidi.

And then there was Pauline's jewellery, two boxes of it. She had never had a wedding ring, nor an engagement ring, any more than I had, but she had plenty of stuff nevertheless. I imagined that a person wearing all of it at the same time, besides looking like a Christmas tree would fall to the floor under the weight of it all. Strings of beads and gems and gold and silver for neck and arms, enough earrings and rings to start a shop, and I had no notion of how to know which bits were expensive and which had come from Woolworths. Again I thought of Heidi – this was rightfully hers but I hadn't been going to let

Gavin anywhere near it. Now that he was gone I should discuss it with Heidi but at the moment that wasn't possible. We weren't speaking.

Now, these days, Heidi phones me every day. Like me, because of that stupid Ros, she, and Jojo and the children, and Adam, are forbidden to go out, even to the shops. She has her shopping delivered – five people, three meals a day, equals quite a load. It falls on Jarvis to bring any small items that have been forgotten from the order, and he also brings me what I need. He puts a couple of bags on the doorstep, rings the bell and retreats to the front gate. I open the door and call out my news. ('Fine. No problem. You all right?' 'Yeah. Good.' 'How's the baby? Paige OK?') Then I go inside, look at the receipt and send him the money by using my phone. Human interaction it isn't.

They were so much older than us, Maureen and Barbara; they were born before the war and it might have been a different country. They remembered seeing the red glow in the sky as fires burned in London, they had seen a plane pitching into the North Sea, they remembered rationing and the time when there was a King instead of a Queen. They left school at fourteen and went to work – that would be like sending Jarvis out to work, pale and quiet and scared in some factory full of noise and unintelligible demands.

Poor Barbara, the family always said. She was just sixteen when she carried either me or my sister through the cold dark waters and saw our mother swept away to her death. Before she was seventeen she had got pregnant, got married to Brian and moved out of the family home, which was being slowly dried out and restored. Then – of course We were too young to know this at the time – she had a late miscarriage and, so it was said in the family, was never the same after that. I take it to mean that she was once, as a girl, of a more sunny and optimistic disposition, but then, weren't we all. Or maybe they mean that she was easier to push around, or that she accepted what people said to her without looking for the flaws in their pronouncements. She and Brian had a couple of daughters in the end; We knew them well, though they were a bit too young for us to want to play with them.

We liked Brian when We were young. He called us Twinkles and seemed always to have sweets in his pocket. A charmer, they say in the family when Barbara isn't around, and the implication is that he was charming to rather too many people, and before the girls were teenagers she had divorced him. Even his own daughters found him more pleasant than their mother and eventually, when they were teenagers, went to live with him and his second wife. None of this improved Barbara.

'Poor Barbara,' Pauline used to say. 'She brought those girls up single-handed and they were a credit to her, and Brian more or less enticed them away from her. It makes me glad,' she would add sometimes, 'that Heidi *doesn't* know her father.'

Poor Barbara, however, being quite clever and conscientious, did well for herself. Instead of staying in factory work she learned shorthand and typing and became, I believe, one of those people without whom a given office cannot function. Maureen, once her children were in school, worked at the same electrical factory but on the shop floor, not letting on to her workmates that her little sister worked Upstairs, on a monthly salary, not a weekly wage.

'So what have you been doing with yourself?' said Maureen.

Barbara was still a bit cool with me and not saying much.

'Working,' I said.

'You must have some time off,' she said. 'Weekends.'

So I told them I was researching the Dale Dyke Dam Disaster for the Historical Society and they were suitably impressed.

'Well, I've never heard of that before,' said Maureen. 'Even when we've been here before – you'd think they'd make something of it, big event like that.'

Maureen had always been conscientious about visiting; when Dennis was still capable they would drive up nearly every year to spend a few days with us. They stayed at Pauline's then, she being a better cook and a more practised hostess. She made meals, I just turned up with drink. Barbara had rarely been; maybe because having divorced her husband long ago she felt she had no one to accompany her, maybe she just didn't want that much to see us. She sat a little further away from me than Maureen did, looking through my book, The Collapse of the Dale Dyke Dam by Geoffrey Amey, examining the pictures.

'Well of course,' she said then, 'that's what you'd expect. That's what Canvey looked like, though *you* can't remember it.'

'I know,' I said. I always felt – We always felt – at a disadvantage to the rest of the family. Even Alan had memories of the flood and our mother, and We didn't, however much We tried. Even so, We felt – both of us, not only me – like experts on floods. Her dreams, Pauline's, when she told them to me, were about water . . . And mine were not. Why should We have had different dreams? It seemed wrong.

'I'm not sure,' said Maureen, 'that it's such a good idea, this flood thing. You don't want to be getting morbid.' And before I could read her some stories from Harrison's book – which was my favourite – she turned the subject to Heidi and her family and I had to admit that I hadn't seen them lately.

'Such a nice boy,' she said, 'that Jarvis. Nice polite boy.'

Maureen had a son and two daughters, all of whom I had known well when we were all young, and they of course had children and, now, grandchildren. There was enough there to talk about without having to bring Heidi into it. She started telling us about a boy called Reuben – I was supposed to know who he was and it took a while to find out that he was her great-grandson – who was being tested for being autistic. 'Like Heidi's boy,' she said.

'Jojo?' I said. 'He's not autistic. Whatever is wrong with his brain doesn't have a name. It's not a syndrome or anything, it's just neo-natal brain damage, that's what we've always been told.'

'I haven't seen him since he was a little tot,' she said. 'I remember him being slow to walk and talk and so on. She just had the two then, quite close together. And she's got a couple more now, I remember seeing the little girl, last time I was up here with Dennis. She'll have changed a bit by now.'

'At least there's no twins,' said Barbara.

'What's wrong with being twins?'

'You wouldn't know of course, would you, being just on the receiving end, so to speak. It was me and Maureen who came in for the job of looking after you two.' She went into what I suppose was her mum's – our mum's – voice: 'You Bar, get them babies out of here before I give em what for. Didn't we Mo.'

'Oh we did,' said Maureen. 'Feeding, changing nappies, pushing you round to try to get you off to sleep. And then one of you would wake the other one up. Double trouble weren't you.'

'What I can't believe,' said Barbara, 'is that we went and had our own babies, you'd think we'd have known better.'

'It was normal wasn't it. All our mates did it. After the war you couldn't walk down the street for tripping over toddlers. Everyone had a couple of kids, till they found out what was causing it.'

'Four though,' said Barbara, returning to Heidi, 'Not many have four these days.'

She was clearly disapproving and I felt like I wanted to defend Heidi, however much I might have wanted to agree.

'She manages all right,' I said.

'But she must miss her mum,' said Barbara, and Maureen got going then with how wonderful her mum had been, what a support, nothing was too much for her. Et cetera.

I could hear her name by that time. It had been said to me in conversations at school so often that I no longer shied away like some panic-struck horse when I heard it. I could think it and even say it, though not without some sort of internal jolt. But my sisters – my remaining sisters – were taking it a bit too far for comfort. Pauline this and Pauline that, and Do you remember Pauline when, and Pauline always. . .

I broke into their reminiscences to tell them that Heidi's bloke had upped and gone but as a diversion it didn't work. 'She'll miss her mum more than ever.' 'Poor thing, it's no time to be left on your own.' 'It's lucky for her she's got you then, Pammy.'

'For god's sake,' I said, but Maureen took it as an exclamation of modesty on my part.

'I know,' she said. 'I know what you mean. It's part of god's plan.' (I hadn't known till that moment that she'd caught a bit of religion off that Home where Dennis was kept.) 'The lord taketh away and the lord giveth back,' she added, which didn't sound right to me, but what did I know.

'When the lord see-eth fit,' said Barbara caustically, and I interrupted to ask if they'd like more tea, or something stronger.

We didn't as a rule do religion in our family. Weddings and funerals maybe or maybe not, but not christenings and certainly not churchgoing on a regular basis. As I put cups and saucers (!) and a milk jug (!) on a tray in the kitchen I could hear Barbara saying that it was a lot of mumbo-jumbo and Maureen saying that the people were so nice, so friendly, so caring, and there was no harm in a bit of comfort.

'They'll get their hooks into you,' said Barbara. 'You know they will, and they won't let go and before you know it you'll be up at that church hall behind the tea urn and they'll be asking you for all your money. I know you, and I know what they're like.'

'You should come too,' said Maureen. 'They'd love to meet you.'

'In your dreams,' said Barbara, which made me smile as I could tell from the relish she said it with that it was a phrase she'd picked up off her grandchildren.

She came into the kitchen to help. 'Pauline didn't go to church did she?'

'No,' I said.

'Of course not,' she said. 'Her funeral wasn't churchy at all. I thought it was lovely, just as she would have wanted it. Not churchy at all,' She raised her voice for the last bit to make sure Maureen would hear.

Our nan used to send us to Sunday school; Alan had the job of getting us there and back but there were no big roads to cross and hardly any traffic. He was five or six then and he held a hand of each of us the way Nan told him to and looked both ways at the kerbs. We were tiny then – she just wanted an afternoon off, a couple of hours to put her feet up and look through the News of the World headlines and look to see if Leyton Orient had won or not.

At the Sunday school we were in a different room from Alan, what they called the baby room, where two of what we thought were teachers but in fact must have been a couple of schoolgirls stood and gossiped together while we coloured in pictures, and then made us sing I'm H-A-P-P-Y and another song. The other song was our favourite; We sang it at home to Nan until she told us to pack it in, and then We sang it to each other in the back yard, in the street, in our bedroom, laughing fit to wet our knickers. We just thought it was funny. I can't remember now what all the words were; I just know it ended up, You in your small corner, and I in mine. And We would crouch down very small and then spring up, joyous and giggling. Ah yes, We made our own amusements, in ways that would have been beyond, say, Heidi's Cassie, but then, Cassie hasn't got the benefit of a twin sister.

They sat there, my only remaining sisters, nibbling at cake (shop-bought) and sipping at white wine (Barbara had looked critically at the label, but managed to force herself to drink it) and embarked upon telling me about poor Alan.

'He ought to retire.'

'It's a lot of stress.'

'Being married to Alison doesn't help.'

'She won't want him to retire, she likes her holidays too much.'

'And her lifestyle.'

'Nothing but the best for Alison.'

'And he's still got to support Bradley.'

'What's Bradley doing now,' I asked.

'He wants to go to Art College now. He thinks he could make it as a fashion designer.'

I huffed crossly because Bradley had tried every way he could come up with of acquiring money by being famous, but had so far not found anything he could be famous for, at least not without some effort on his part. We all knew Alan would be too soft to tell him to leave home and stand on his own two feet.

'You see,' said Maureen, 'Alan hangs on to Alison and does what she wants because he lost his mother so young. It's psychological.'

'You don't know that,' said Barbara. 'Vin lost his mother as well, but he never let a wife boss him about.'

'He never had a wife. Anyway,' Maureen sipped her wine and dabbed her eyes, 'they were both terribly affected by it.'

I opened my mouth to say something but Barbara spoke before I got the words out. 'You and Pauline were all right. You were too young to notice. Too young to understand.'

'It was a blessing,' said Maureen. 'Poor little mites, you wouldn't want them to understand.'

'Some people have it easy,' said Barbara, 'and some get the rough end of the stick. Of course we wouldn't wish on you and Pauline, what we had to go through.'

'That's good of you,' I said. 'I'm sure that's very good of you.'

'You've got very bitter,' said Maureen. She said it sadly, like a description rather than an accusation, but Barbara's tone was more hostile.

'She's always been bitter,' she said, as though I wasn't there. 'She's always known Pauline was better than her. More – more everything.'

'More clever?' I said. (My A levels had been impressive, hers had only just scraped her into college.) 'More sensible?' (*I* hadn't gone and had a baby without any support from whoever its father was.)

'She only means,' said Maureen, 'that Pauline was a bit – easier, maybe.'

'Better with people,' said Barbara. 'Not so prone to upset people.'

'Like you I suppose,' I said.

I couldn't even throw her out of my house. I would have had to drive her to the station and she would probably have wait there till morning for a train. Not that I didn't consider it.

'Are we going to see Heidi this morning?' they asked at breakfast.

'She'll be doing her big weekly shop,' I lied. I hadn't yet mentioned that she was not speaking to me. 'I'll take you to see the dam this morning and you can see Heidi this afternoon.' By then, I hoped, I would have found a way round the situation.

'Of course,' said Maureen – this seemed to be what they had been talking about over their cup-of-tea-in-bed – 'Nan was upset when you two went to live with Vi. There were proper arguments about it I can tell you. All through the family, some of them saying one thing and some of them saying another. Our dad didn't know what to do. You'd just about got to an age where you could be useful. You could have looked after Nan, you only had a year of school left to do, you could have taken the load off of her, you could have shopped and cooked and done the washing and the cleaning and she could have had a rest. Goodness knows she deserved a rest.'

'She was agreeable,' said Barbara. 'She agreed to them going to Vi's. She knew it was the best thing for them, in her heart she knew it.'

'She might have said so,' said Maureen. 'She wasn't going to stand in their way, she said. But she missed them all the same. If they'd have visited more often – but they had their homework to do, Vi always said.'

I don't think We ever gave a thought to what Nan felt about us leaving. We knew that We were nuisances because she told us so, but We also knew that she loved us. When she wasn't feeling harried and hurried by our demands she used to sing to us. Probably her voice wasn't up to much but We didn't mind because she had a song that We believed was ours and ours only. "You are my Honeysuckle" it was called, and contained the lines 'I love you Dearly Dearly' which We always heard with capital letters. It was our name! In a song! And not once but twice, because there were two of us. She didn't sing it every day but if she was in a good mood when We went to bed she would come and tuck us in and sing it to us, sitting on the side of the bed, making a big dip in the mattress which one of us – whoever was nearest that side – would try to squeeze into.

'I love you dearly, dearly, and I want you to love me,' she sang, and tapped her cigarette ash into our chamber pot which We had because the toilet was downstairs and out the back. She did want us to love her – We knew for sure she loved us because didn't she give ten years of her life to us when she could have been pottering around peacefully instead of keeping us in clean clothes and having us complain about having liver for our tea. Didn't she give up her bed to us and sleep on the sofa until We left and went to Vi's. Didn't she send Alan to us to invite us to tea on Sundays, and didn't We say We would go and then find that some other outing was more attractive.

We did love her – she wanted us to and We did but We still went and left her and after a bit I don't think We missed her.

We never loved Violet and I don't believe she ever loved us. She found Pauline easier to get along with because she was more domesticated and outwardly at least – reasonable. More house-trained. To each other, in bed at night, We whispered how We hated being there, hated our new school, how We were going to run away back to Nan. But We never got round to it and then before very long Nan died and our dad sold her little house and Alan went back to Canvey to live with him.

'She did a good job, Vi did,' said Barbara. 'They would never have got on like they did without her. They would have turned into little sluts and got married at sixteen like you and me did.'

I drove them up to Thornseats. It was a pleasant enough day and they were well wrapped up against the cold that they believed was Sheffield's constant climate. I knew better than to expect them to walk more than a hundred yards, but that was all it took to get to the Clob stone.

CLOB – carved on a stone about half the size of a loaf of bread. It stands for Centre Line of Old Barrier and from it you can see the new dam, some way upstream, constructed on a firmer foundation and on a stricter specification.

'That's it?' they said. They looked around them as if searching for the information centre, or the gift shop.

I pointed out the tiny commemorative plaque on the floor.

'Call *that* a memorial?'

'*How* many people did you say? That died?'

'About two hundred and forty. Plus the ones that never recovered and died later.'

'You'd think,' said Barbara, 'that people round here, or the council, or someone, could come up with something a bit bigger than that.'

'We've got one in Canvey,' said Maureen. 'By the library, lovely new plaque, all the names on it. I always stop and read it when I'm over there.'

'It's a disgrace,' said Barbara, 'not to have something better than that. Poor people I suppose, no one to stick up for them.'

I felt as if it was my fault, even as I agreed with them. Since then, down in town, next to the Don, they have installed a neat, stylish, modern stone inscribed with the names. I've seen it, but somehow the old Clob stone is more evocative.

I took them for coffee and cake in Bradfield and it was still only half past ten when they were pecking like hens at the last crumbs.

'Are there any shops?' said Barbara. They can walk miles if there is saleable stuff to look at, no trouble, so I drove them to Bakewell and they had a nice time poking round the gift shops and the charity shops and we had lunch in a café.

'What about –' said Maureen, and then lowered her voice so that I had to ask her to say it again, louder.

'Ashes,' she said. 'Pauline's ashes?'

'Heidi's got them,' I said, 'as far as I know. Unless they're still at the funeral place.'

'And what's going to happen? Because we would like to be there, all of us?'

I had never considered that possibility. 'I don't know. I haven't discussed it with her. Not yet.' I did not know if I would ever be able to.

'We can ask her when we see her this afternoon.'

Barbara took out her phone. 'What time will I say to her?'

'Who?'

'Heidi. I'm calling to remind her that we're going round there this afternoon, aren't I.'

I dithered.

'Well,' she said sharply, 'how long will it take to get back there from here?'

'Thirty minutes, maybe forty, depends on the traffic.'

'I'll tell her half past two,' she said decisively.

I whispered to Maureen, 'I'll have to drop you off and come back for you. Things are a bit –'

'Speak a bit louder dear,' she said.

'Never mind.'

Barbara said, 'She didn't seem to know we were up here at all. But it's all right, she'll be at home all afternoon.'

'I'll have to drop you off and pick you up later,' I said. 'I'll be getting our dinner ready.' It was one of Pauline's casseroles which had been in my freezer and was already defrosted and ready to go, but I wasn't going to go into details.

'I thought you would come with us,' said Barbara, but Maureen patted my arm and said, 'That will be fine. You'll be needing a little rest from us.'

After I had dropped them off I went home and smoked the cigarette that I would have had in the morning if I hadn't been avoiding their disapproval. It was peaceful, standing at the back door, seeing the sun break though the clouds. I took a small walk through the garden, thinking I should get out there and dead head the daffodils but I remembered I had to prepare the vegetables and went indoors. It doesn't take long to peel a few potatoes and extract a packet of frozen peas from the freezer. The feeling of relief that I no longer had my big sisters scrutinising my life faded and I was almost looking forward to their return. I turned the oven on, and the phone rang.

'We're staying here at Heidi's for our evening meal,' said Barbara. Maureen would have apologised. 'She says you can come over too if you like.'

'No thank you,' I said, too quickly. 'Just call me when you're ready to come home. I'll come and get you.'

'It's all right,' said Barbara. 'Heidi says she'll drive us over, you don't need to bother.'

'Fine,' I said.

I turned the oven off and put the casserole in the fridge. I would not spend my evening thinking of them talking to Heidi and exclaiming over the cuteness of the little children; I would do something useful and I would eat toast. As many slices of toast as I wanted. And smoke another fag.

Of course I had to wait up until they came back and they were full of it – what a good mother, what lovely children, even Jojo ('can't help it poor soul') came in for his share.

'She asked after you,' said Maureen.

'She said you'd had a few words,' said Barbara.

'You mustn't be hard on her,' said Maureen. 'She's having a hard time.'

'She's a motherless child,' said Barbara.

'Like we all are,' said Maureen.

'She thought the world of those children,' said Barbara. *She* meaning Pauline.

'Well,' said Maureen, 'the thing is, she had a lot of love to give.'

And I don't, is what you're saying. Of course I didn't say it out loud; even I have some social skill sometimes. But I thought it, and it seemed true to me. Although – how does anyone know that what they are feeling, what they believe is love, is the same thing that someone else is feeling.

I didn't argue, but when they had gone to bed and I was standing outside the back door sending a thin ghost of smoke into the air, I recalled how Pauline used to tell me, when we were kids, that she dreamed about our mother and the first time I pretended I hadn't heard her, and then pretended she hadn't said it, but a few days, or weeks, later she said it again and I had to ask, What was she like? And she said, Nice, which told me nothing. We always assumed that our mother was nice. Alan, when we asked him, said she was fat.

'Was she nice though?'

'Um yeah, she was nice.'

'Nicer than Dad?'

He shrugged and turned away. Whether she was nice or not, We eventually realised, he missed her more than We did.

Barbara's words came back to me – a motherless child. That's what it's like now I thought. I never felt it before but now, I feel like a motherless child.

By the end of Sunday afternoon they were safely on their way home, more than halfway I calculated. Alan had promised to pick them up at King's Cross and take them to their separate homes.

'He's a good man,' said Maureen.

'Shame about his wife,' said Barbara. Something we agreed on, me and her.

'Of course,' wittered Maureen, 'Jimmy would have come to fetch us if it wasn't for his hip. Or Edward would but he's in the Canary Islands.'

'Lucky you've got three brothers then,' I said, thinking, What about me? Who will there be for me to fall back on when I have to stop driving?

Maureen must have read my mind. 'And you've got Heidi and her boys to look after you,' she said.

I ignored her though I could have said it would be a miraculous day when Jojo could look after anyone at all, and the baby wasn't a year old yet, and anyway, why wasn't she including Cassie – did she think girls weren't able to drive? The efforts I had been making to watch my tongue had made me tired; all I wanted now was for them to go home and leave me in peace.

Barbara shed some more tears over Pauline when she said goodbye to me, and Maureen looked anxious – no one ever wanted Barbara to have an emotional episode again. They hugged me and said what I suppose were nice things, and trundled away into the station.

I was quite pleased that I had remained brisk and practical throughout the visit, but at the same time I knew they would have been thinking I didn't care enough.

'We're lucky we've still got you,' said Maureen, on her way up the stairs on Saturday night, but she was wrong. They had not got me, because I was nothing without Pauline. It was like cutting an arm and a leg off someone, and a sizeable portion of head, and telling them they can still compete in a heptathlon, they can still win Strictly, they can still walk down the street without people feeling sorry for them. 'Only six of us left now,' said Maureen, and I wanted to scream, but didn't.

The daffodils are over so I go in to the garden – still can't call it *my* garden – and pinch off the dead heads. They are not to my taste, these daffs, I prefer something smaller, more delicate, less strident but she would always go for the ones with the biggest muscles and the most insistent yellow. I could have dug them up any time over the years I've lived here but have never felt I had the right. Or else that I would regret it if I did, as if I would have lost another bit of her. So they come up every year, front garden and back, multiplying every year and occasionally a neighbour will pause and look at them and say something like 'Don't they cheer you up.' No, they don't.

Today – strictly speaking tomorrow – I am out of quarantine. I have had no symptoms of the virus, though plenty of symptoms of mental breakdown. Rage, at almost anything, enough handwashing to get me diagnosed with OCD, an irrational fear of leaving the house, now that I am able to do it. Boiling fury at bloody Ros, whose 'cough' has apparently come to nothing.

Heidi, to do her justice, has phoned me every day and whatever else it has done it has made me grateful not to be in that house with all of them. It seems that Jordan is the least bothered by having to stay at home; the two teenagers have been sleeping for unfeasible amounts of time during the day and staying up most of the night connected to screens and headphones. 'One good thing,' says Heidi. 'They seem to get on quite well together. For the first time ever.'

They can all be allowed out now, but only for exercise once a day. Adam is working from home, though how he can survey the roads and bridges of Sheffield from there I do not understand. 'He's got reports to write,' says Heidi. Her workplace – the special school where Jojo used to go – is closed for the duration.

So all she has to keep her busy is phoning round the family – if Marconi, or whoever, had never invented the telephone I swear the Dearlys would have had to do it for him. So, every day she calls Jarvis and Paige, Adam's mother, me, and some old lady down in Chapeltown on her old street. She also has a rota which takes in the Essex branches of the family. She asks if I have spoken to Alan, which of course I have. Likewise Barbara and Verona. She has nothing to say that I haven't already heard but she tells me anyway. I should be grateful. I'm not.

She tells me the latest news about Pollyanna, which however is not extensive given that she's only two weeks old. Jarvis and Paige and the baby are fine, is the only news. Of course Jarv's garden centre has had to close but he will be paid by some government scheme; Paige is on maternity leave anyway. They send photos everyday to Heidi, and now that Cassie and Jayden are out of quarantine they will be able to go shopping for all of us. I would prefer to do my shopping myself, once I get up the courage to go out.

'I wish you could come round and see us,' says Heidi. 'I wish we could celebrate being allowed out again.'

But we both know that under the new rules I should not go in anyone else's home. Normally I wouldn't care to anyway, but now it feels like a major deprivation.

River Loxley to Malin Bridge

CSE Local History
Dale Dyke Dam Disaster
Worksheet 4

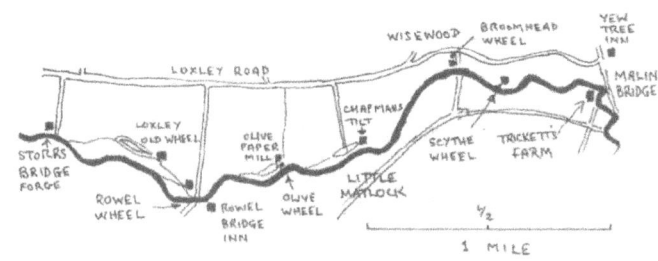

1. Copy the map of the River Loxley and mark and label the water mills.

2. Write down as many products as you can that the mills and factories were producing

I had not the smallest idea that would make sense of why I was doing this, but that seemed to be how life was at that time. The world went on, I got up, I ate and drank and went to work, I even spoke, I even laughed on occasion, and at no point could I have said why I was doing these things. I hadn't seen Terry – in fact I had avoided the Ramblers so that I didn't have to see him. I had decided against having this project to complete and yet I was still plodding down the Loxley valley as if it meant something.

"The flood waters lifted a cart with a load of three tons of coal and swept it down and into the mill where Joseph Denton drowned and his little brother John saved himself by climbing a pole and hanging on for half an hour until the water level dropped.

William Chapman was almost held by his father as the water tried to suck him through a window – but a beam fell on the father's head and he lost his grip, and so William drowned, like the other Chapmans, Daniel and Ellen and their two little boys, along with their maid and two apprentices."

It was a rare sunny day when I walked down along the Loxley River. People were out with their dogs and their children, the river was brown and full, birds made springtime sort of noises in bushes and trees and you could almost see the leaves unfolding as you watched. If Pauline had been there she would have mentioned how much she loved the spring, how lovely it was to see the sun on the leaves, how it was all like a new beginning, how we were so lucky to live where there were footpaths and rivers. Et cetera. And I would have said something like, You always say that, as if I was dismissing her unoriginal opinions, or I would have pointed out that she rarely walked for longer than fifteen minutes – round the block with Vinny the dog. And she would have said I was grouchy or curmudgeonly and neither of us would have been offended.

There is not much to see along the Loxley except for trees and water. The steep hill on the Stannington side and the gentler slope in the other direction. Of course the bulk of Stannington would not have been imagined in 1864, let alone built. Beside the river there are bits of remains of works and mills – stumps of masonry and silted up ponds – but you would have to be a better historian that I am, or a different sort of historian, to be able to know what they are. There were books in the library that I could use for researching such things but I knew I wouldn't. Getting out my old school material had shown me how patchy and superficial it was, and I knew I did not have the energy to improve it. History changed with the coming of the National Curriculum; nowadays it was the causes of the Second World War; it was about the despised and mistreated people of the world; it was about, This must never happen again, as though it was not still going on in front of our eyes and noses.

There was a field with a few sheep, there were people walking dogs, and then, after you pass the sheltered housing complex for well-off old people, you get to Malin Bridge.

Malin Bridge was and still is a nondescript, scruffy little place of small shops, a factory, a pub or two and a few houses, some of them looking unloved. The centre of it is effectively a traffic island where five or six roads converge, roads which will take you back to Bradfield, or to Stannington, or Hillsborough or out towards the Manchester Road into Derbyshire or up over the hill to Wisewood. When I brought the kids here – the Year 10s – they were relieved to get back into civilisation and some of them knew where they were, but there was nothing historically remarkable to look at.

"The flood, having swept down the valley with little to stop it, slammed into the village of Malin Bridge with great force."

But Miss, water doesn't hurt you. Every year someone would say that. The wave machine at Hillsborough Baths was the nearest they'd been to any water-related danger.

I would try to make sense. Say someone poured a pint of water over your head. You'd be offended, sure, affronted and cross, and wet. But not hurt. Say they threw the water at you, all at once. Would that hurt? A pint of water weighs a pound. A gallon would therefore weigh eight pounds – think four bags of flour. Would that hurt if it hit you all of a sudden? I couldn't be sure but it seemed likely. Then think of the millions of gallons released by the breach in the dam. Think of the gallon at the front of the charge with the weight of the other umpteen millions behind it. That would do some damage.

I suppose, they'd say.

More than a hundred people lost their lives in the next half hour, I would tell the kids. I would show them a picture then, a photograph of the Cleakum pub on the morning after the flood. The chimney of the public house is still standing; one window remains in place, and a small sliver of roof. There are no floors, there is no furniture, no beds. Five children were sleeping in their beds; it was almost midnight so their parents too might have finished clearing the bar after the evening's work and also have been in bed. All of the seven were drowned. Bisby was their name and it is a name you can still find in the Sheffield phone book.

Across the road from the Cleakum was the Stag. 'Twelve people,' I used to tell the children, 'twelve from the same family, were washed out of a pub that stood there, and drowned. Plus three others who were staying there.' I could tell them their names, their ages. They would go quiet, briefly.

The Cleakum was rebuilt and called the Malin Bridge Inn but the Stag never was. Maybe there was no one who believed it would be worth it. Now there's Burgon and Balls factory, where they make secateurs and such. I have a pair.

Of course, there was only so much water that came down. It was not the same sort of flood as when a river rises and stays spread over fields for weeks because there is nowhere for it to go. This water had somewhere to go – downhill, southeast, down the Loxley, joining with the Rivelin, joining with the Don, through the town, carrying with it all the stones and machinery from the workshops, the beds and tables from the houses, the horses and livestock from the farms and smallholdings, and the dead and dying people, until the reservoir was empty. Then the water stopped coming. The photos showed what it left behind. Heaps of stone. Dead horses. Houses that look as if they had been bombed. People standing about, looking, not comprehending maybe what had happened. How could this be, this destruction, when the water was gone, like a Biblical visitation.

I stood there, looking over the bridge through the bushes at the water flowing peaceably – a bit high perhaps. It had been a wet winter and a late spring, but I wasn't any sort of expert on river levels so it looked fine to me.

Once you get to Malin Bridge there is no more walking beside the river. It now runs behind Burgon and Balls, behind the Towsure shop and a long row of little terraced houses, some of which are now turned into shops – decidedly non-thriving shops to judge from the outside. Back in 1864 there were half a dozen water-powered mills between here and where the river met the Don at Owlerton. I parked near the tram stop one afternoon after school and walked towards Hillsborough on Holme Lane. It's not something you would put in a guided walk – traffic, tramlines, smallness. If I ever came to write the walk up I would advise getting the tram into Hillsborough, never mind looking here for anything historical.

What is History for? No one ever asked me and I never asked myself. Sure, sometimes some bolshie kid would look up from his or her exercise book and say, What are we learning this crap for? but I never had to make a serious attempt at answering.

I taught History because it was my main subject at teacher training college. It was my main subject because it was the one I did best in at A level. I took it for A level because it was one of my best O levels and because I liked the teacher. It was one of my best O levels because I had a good memory and I liked stories. That is the history of me and history. I never gave a thought to what it was for. Probably at the beginning of teacher training – I say probably, I could be wrong – we were asked to offer some sort of explanation for the study of history and the reasons for inflicting it, in its evolving forms, on children, and I probably said, with all the others, that it was the way to understand ourselves and our times. But when I consider Jarvis and Cassie and even Jayden, I wonder if that can be true: they seems to understand something about the times they live in better than I do, yet their knowledge of history, as per the current curriculum, is minimal, muddled, Anglo-centric and restricted.

The reason I liked teaching *local* history and thought it was a Good Thing was that there was a connection between it and the pupils. We called them pupils in those days, not students – there's another bit of history. But if you could show them – I mean stand in a group and point to a real something, the Cholera Monument, the bear pit in the Botanical Gardens, the CLOB stone, the Hillsborough Barracks which were built to put down political riots, the stone dragon over the door of the Town Hall and the frieze of trades above it – surely if they see these things with their own eyes, even if it's all a laugh and an excuse to go out in the minibus, surely they begin to form an idea of the city they live in, how it was made and how it has made them. And if they come from somewhere else – Bangladesh or Pakistan or Poland – then there's even more reason.

If I ever gave it any thought at all I'd probably say it was good for them to feel that they belong to this place, and know something about it, and can pass something on to their children. And that probably felt important to me because We *didn't* belong. We didn't belong in Sheffield – our accent and our lack of understanding of the North proved it. And more than that, We didn't belong in South Benfleet with Nan, or in Leigh-on-Sea with Auntie Vi, not because other people said so but because We felt, and talked about it often, that We should be back in Canvey with our dad and our oldest brothers and sisters. It was ridiculous because We had, as I say, no memories of living there, no memories of our mother or the time before the flood, but as teenagers We told ourselves the story that Canvey was home and that We were a long way from it, not in miles but in belonging.

Of course I know that it changes; the past changes as the present changes. Practices that were once upon a time normal, and even laudable – burning Catholics comes to mind – would be frowned on now, looked at squeamishly with modern eyes. Even the words. I remember the terms my father – and Nan, and Auntie Vi, all of us – used to talk about people who were not as English as we were, the words teachers used to use to describe a child who wasn't paying attention or was failing to understand the twelve times table. How much worse it must have been a hundred years before that. How little they were thought of, those families whose livelihood was swept away, whose children were drowned and whose houses buckled and fell apart under the weight of water.

Allowing, or forcing, poor people to live in badly built houses that crumpled under the weight of water from the dam while the stone built houses of the better-off were more likely to remain standing was one of the scandals revealed by the flood, though probably not much has changed, in the relative terms of rich and poor. The thing that talks is still the money, and if you have it you are assumed to deserve it. As I assume that I have what I have because somehow I deserve it.

I spent some time that holiday in my sister's garden. I would have had plenty to do in mine but I told myself I was helping to attract and convince prospective buyers. Mine could wait, there was only me to care about it, whatever Jarvis said, and anyway, Pauline's was the sort of garden that looked much worse when it was neglected. Mine was larger, but crowded with plants – at this time of the year all growing like weeds so that the actual weeds were barely noticeable. Pauline on the other hand, had neat borders with space between the plants, where weeds would soon get a hold if left. Anyway, I wanted to be there, not because I liked it but because I knew that very soon, as soon as it was sold I would no longer be able to have even that faint contact with her.

I dead-headed her early daffodils and I pruned her two rose bushes that grew up against the fence. It seemed to make her garden even more naked and bleak. I began to pull out the groundsel and herb Robert and the occasional dandelion, knowing that more of them would only grow as soon as I turned my back. I heard a noise behind me, a sort of tentative throat-clearing. There was a man there, a short elderly man in a cagoule and a beanie hat.

'I hope I didn't startle you,' he said.

'Not at all,' I said.

'You must be Pamela,' he said.

'And you are?'

'Sorry. Of course you don't know me. I'm Trevor. Trev Philp. I'm a friend of Pauline. Was. I saw the side gate was open and I thought I would just pop in, just to check everything was shut up properly round the back. I hope I didn't –'

'No you didn't,' I said. I stood up.

'Grass needs cutting,' he said. 'I suppose Barry hasn't –?'

'No he hasn't,' I said. 'It's too wet anyway. When it dries out a bit I'll do it.'

'If you need any help –'

'I don't think so,' I said.

'I'm sorry I disturbed you.'

'No problem,' I said. I had not looked him in the eye at all and I thought he would go but he came further into the garden and began to inspect the pruning I'd done on the roses.

'Lovely rose, this one,' he said. 'The Pilgrim. Yellow. Goes on right through the autumn.'

'I know,' I said.

'Though if I was her I wouldn't have put a red one next to it.'

'Me neither.'

He took his rucksack off and sat down on the bench. 'Want some chocolate?'

Ah well. Like truffles to a pig. I sat beside him and we talked about plants. He told me about his flat where he had a balcony so full of potted plants that his neighbours worried the whole structure would collapse. I told him that my raspberries were very late showing any new leaves and that I wished it was the time of year for taking some cuttings from Pauline's garden.

'I've got a plant of that choisya,' he said, pointing at it. 'I mean it grew from a cutting of hers. I can take one later in the year and grow it on for you.'

'Of course,' I said, 'if the house doesn't sell quickly I may be able to get some.'

'Your garden is bigger I believe.'

'Bigger and scruffier,' I said. 'The weather hasn't been on our side this year.'

'I miss this garden,' he said. 'I mean, I miss mine, that I had to leave behind, and now I feel like I've lost this one too. Even though it wasn't mine in any way. Not my style really.'

'What was your garden like? Your own garden?'

He thought for a bit. 'I suppose you would say it was a man's garden,' he said. 'I had crazes. Collections. I would take a notion to have a bed full of species peonies, dig it all out and spend money on buying all the different varieties I could find. Then get bored with it a year or two later. Go in for sweet peas or whatever.'

'I wouldn't like that,' I said. 'I like a bit of everything.'

'The last thing I did with it,' he said, 'was to turn it all over to shrubs. Wanted to have a topiary garden. Just green shapes, nothing else, no colour except green. My wife didn't like it,' he said. 'Not that that was the only thing she didn't like.'

I didn't ask him what else. I didn't want to know. After a small silence he said, 'How's the family?'

'What? Heidi? Do you know Heidi?'

'I've met her of course. But Jarvis. How's Jarvis?'

'Not too bad.'

'Sensitive boy,' he said. 'And very fond of his Granma. It must be hard for him. For you as well.'

'We're managing,' I said. Then remembered how my sisters would tell me off for being rude and tried to be a bit nicer. 'How did you know Pauline? Are you a teacher?'

'Retired,' he said. 'We worked together years ago. Same department. One of those times when Art came under Technology, and so did Home Ec.'

'Art's in with Music now,' I said. 'At our school anyway. So you were an Art teacher. Do you paint?'

He shrugged. 'Do a bit here and there. You need a bit of enthusiasm to get you going, don't you find. Sure I'd feel better if I did but I don't seem to get going.' He paused for a long time and then said. 'I do miss her – Pauline.'

'Were you –' I didn't know what word to use.

'Not really. Just friends. But close friends I would say. Not a romance, though I have to admit I did think about it. But I think friends was enough for her.'

'Did she say so?'

'Never asked her. Did she say anything to you?'

'I never knew of your existence. Until Jarvis mentioned your name. I think he was missing you a bit.' I too thought for a while and then said, 'I'm going home for a cup of tea. If you like you can come –'

'Thank you,' he said.

136

We sat in my kitchen. My front room was not fit for anyone to see. I've never been tidy, and lately, with school stuff and Pauline's stuff and empty mugs and sweet wrappers and fag packets on every surface and shoes on the floor along with plates of sandwich crumbs and piles of ancient worksheets – lately it was not fit to be seen, particularly by someone who might think I was as tidy and organised as my sister was. Had been. We drank our tea and tried to make conversation. He put down his empty cup. 'Can I have a look round your garden?' he said.

I felt I had to pretend I was not proud of the state of my garden. 'It's been so wet,' I said, but he was already on his feet and out the back door.

'It's certainly a late spring,' he said, 'but you've got some nice things coming through. Cottage garden kind of style. Not scruffy at all.'

'I suppose,' I said. Some people would have thought it scruffy, but to my mind, and Trev's clearly, it was pretty near perfect – full of the promise of flowers and enough new greenery to suffocate any weeds that might try to find a space.

'And a damson tree,' he said. 'That's nice. Get much fruit?'

'Some years,' I said.

'Make it into jam?'

'Pauline made the jam,' I said, and a great sob came out of my chest, without warning, because Heidi had taken all the jam and I didn't have any.

He pretended not to hear the sob; he turned towards the fence and pulled out a young nettle.

'It'll sting you,' I said.

'Who cares,' he said. 'There are worse things.'

We stood for quite a while in the garden, under a cloudy sky, just looking at the plants and the weeds, discussing, in a barely focussed sort of way, which plants would grow in shade, which colour phlox was the best (his favourite was white, mine was a delicate pink), whether you could ever hope to over-winter a salvia this high up, this far north. Then he thanked me for the tea, asked me to say Hi to Jarvis for him, and left.

The thing about Trev was the fact that he never went anywhere, or visited anywhere, but always 'popped.' It would have irritated me beyond bearing in most people but in other ways he was quite restful so I made a small effort and overlooked it. When I first moved in here he used to pop in quite often at weekends, but when he realised, I guess, that I was never going to make over Pauline's garden, well, I think he gave up on me.

I suppose that to many it is inexplicable that I have never, in all the years I've lived here, made even the smallest attempt to remodel Pauline's garden into something that is more to my liking. There it still is, red and yellow tulips all mixed up together, garishly, like something a three year old would find attractive. Every year I've looked out the back window at them and said to myself, I just let you lot flower this time, then you're coming up. You'll get given away, see if you don't. But it doesn't happen. I nip off the heads when the petals fall, I water them if it's a dry spring, I leave the foliage to wither so as to feed the bulbs for next year. I do the same with the daffodils. I prune the roses, I take off the dead heads; I keep them tidy and ignore the jarring effect of the red and yellow close together. The orange day-lilies have multiplied, and I have let them; a little bit of London Pride has grown into a wide mat which has used up some of the space she used to plant her annuals in.

She mostly relied on seasonal bedding; something that was big and blowsy and colourful would catch her eye in a garden centre and she'd buy three or four, all different colours, and they, by their nature, would not last more than one season. Weeds grow now where her pelargoniums and cosmos clashed. I dig out the dandelions and docks; I pull up the groundsel and goosegrass; I allow forget-me-nots and Welsh poppies to stay and flower, just to cover the ground.

I have never filled the spaces with the sort of planting that I like. Billowing clumps of hardy geraniums, phlox, penstemons; pale colours, whites and pastels – they sometimes invade my mind's eye and I push them away. I know I can't remake my garden in her space. I know it.

The man no longer comes to cut the grass. Jarvis did it for me for a couple of years, but after that he was working and didn't have time. I drag out the mower and trim the lawn but not as often as I could or should. It's mostly daisies by now. The front garden I maintain as it was – three pots, a bay, looking not too bad, and two skimmias, no longer clipped and tidy but straggling and rough and about to break their pots; and a row of her favoured screaming yellow daffodils.

I don't see Trev these days. Haven't done for years really but there are times when something he said will come back to me.

Going back to school after Easter was not as bad as it had been after Christmas. In a sense, and I couldn't blame anyone, Pauline was now in the past. I allowed myself to almost smile at the idea that it had always been me that was Miss Dearly History, but that now she was history. Even I was learning to think of her – sometimes – in the past tense.

For my form group – 11PD – it was their last term. Come September they would be, most of them, at a sixth form in another school in the city, or at the college doing something vocational and – I hoped – suitable to equip them further for grown up life. Only Josh and Kane looked to be heading for being Neets, holding out on the idea that Kerry's brother could get them a job with his girlfriend's uncle. I was not optimistic about their prospects, but on the other hand I was quietly triumphant that Daisy had pulled herself out of her unresponsive mood and had almost caught up with her work and applied to do A levels at the college. I was not going to take credit for the change, not overtly, but I knew that I had put some work in to it and felt a small stirring of satisfaction.

Before they were allowed to stay at home to study, or come in, not in uniform, for revision sessions, or to hang around gossiping in the library, before that – ridiculously to my mind – they would have their school prom. For one thing it was a nasty American idea that forced their parents to spend money they might not have, and for another the prom should happen *after* their exams, not weeks before when it drove everything out of their minds but dresses and hairdos and limousines. I had known people make less fuss over a wedding than these girls did about their prom.

Barbara phoned me. Maureen had already done it, as soon as she got home, giving me details of the journey – the fullness of the train, the anxiety about the cases, the scramble to get the connection, all that. Then she said thank you again for the visit, and I said thank you for coming and we were polite and mendacious and off she went.

Barbara waited a week before she got in touch. She didn't ask how I was, which I suppose I was pleased about, but went straight in to interrogate me about Heidi.

'Have you seen her?' she said. 'Have you made it up with her?'

'We're not children,' I said. 'We don't have to make up.'

'Have you seen her then?'

Of course I hadn't.

'She was right then,' said Barbara. Poisonous cow. 'She said you would never be the one to make up.'

What was this making up idea? When did two grown women have to make up like kids in a playground linking their little fingers and chanting some stupid rhyme?

'She can contact me any time she likes,' I said. 'It was her who put the phone down on me, don't forget that.'

'She invited you. She invited you when we were there; I phoned you and told you. She couldn't have been nicer about it. It was you that said no.'

'She could have asked me herself,' I said. 'She didn't have to get you to do it for her.'

'You're being very stubborn,' said Barbara. 'I told Maureen, I said to her, she'll never make the first move, Pammy won't. Too stubborn. Pauline would never have let her get into this sort of situation. I said to Maureen that you ought to think about what Pauline would have wanted, instead of thinking about yourself all the time.'

'Have you finished?' I was ready to slam the phone down on her.

'You've always been jealous of Heidi,' she said. 'We know all about it, you never wanted to come second with Pauline, even Maureen agrees with me –'

I cut her off then. You can't slam a phone down these days in that satisfying way, but I firmly pressed the button and she was gone. I waited for her to ring again but the rest of that Sunday went by in silence. No doubt she was telling Maureen – and probably Verona and Olive, and certainly Alan – how badly I was behaving.

And sure enough, the following evening, Sunday, Verona called me.

'How *are* you,' she said.

'Fine,' I said.

'School going well?' She was not going to start with Heidi but work round to her more circumspectly.

'Fine,' I said.

'Weather's getting a bit better,' she said.

'Still raining up here,' I said.

'So what are you up to next week?'

I should have said nothing but instead I told her about the Year Eleven prom.

'Lovely,' she said. 'A chance for you to dress up and have a night out.'

I did not point out that I was going to be the one standing on the door at the beginning turning away any young person who was already intoxicated, or who was trying to smuggle in a bottle of vodka, nor that later on in the evening I would be doing regular checks of the girls' toilets on the lookout for cigarettes or spliffs.

'What are you wearing?' she asked.

'Nothing special,' I said. 'Just ordinary school clothes.' And I knew at once that I had released her inner Pauline.

'No,' she said, 'you can't do that. Make an effort, do. You'll be amazed what a difference it makes.'

'No one will care what I look like,' I said.

'You don't do it for other people,' she said. 'You do it for yourself. I thought,' she continued, 'when I saw you back in February, I thought to myself, she's depressed, and who can blame her, but try it, you'll see, you'll feel like a new woman in a nice frock.'

'All right,' I said, thinking to myself, If only you knew how blindingly furious I am about the whole thing – well, certainly you wouldn't talk like this to me if you weren't sitting comfortably a couple of hundred miles away.

It was unexpected, therefore, that I actually found myself getting a suitcase of Pauline's clothes down from the top of the wardrobe and laying some out on the bed.

They stayed there, laid out like bodies, and every evening I went in and looked at them. I knew they would fit me, I didn't need to try anything on, I just looked at them, wondering how I would feel in one of them. After five minutes or so of wondering I came – every evening – to the conclusion that nothing on earth would induce me to even pick one off the bed and I went out and closed the door.

The day before the prom was just the same. In the evening I looked at the dresses, the glossy blue like some exotic bird, the pale pink with darker pink trimmings like a birthday cake, the black and gold like a ceremonial uniform. But black at least which would not seem too out of character for me. I held it up against me and opened the wardrobe to look in the mirror. Too much gold, I could see at once and put it back on the bed.

After school on Thursday I came home to get changed into my best trouser suit, my pale grey one, figuring that something ornamental round my neck would jazz it up quite sufficiently. What I had not remembered was the tomato sauce stain on the lapel – the result of a fish and chip tea in the company of Heidi's children, one I'd meant to get dry-cleaned anyway but had put it off. Other things to think about. My navy blue one I had been wearing all week and I knew what people would think of me; they would know how little I thought of their big night, that for me it was only a duty and I was there only as the alcohol police, rather than to celebrate the ending of their school days. They would be right of course but I still didn't want to be that obvious. That left the black one, which again, of course, everyone had seen on so many occasions – in the classroom, in assemblies, on break duty, dinner duty, detention duty. Even I could see that it did not say Celebration. And I did not want either for people to think I was flaunting my grief as if it was more important than their fun. Although it was.

So, in a hurry now, I went back to Pauline's dresses. Colour was my main criterion as most of their other attributes were lost on me. There was one that was a greeny-blue, or a bluey-green, quite dark in colour, not too fancy; I put it on and decided it would do, a little looser on me than it would have been a few months ago, but I thought that was quite a good thing. I found a pair of tights – they were black-ish but the only ones I had so would have to do; I found my most feminine shoes – they were flat but that was good too, I had no wish to teeter about on high heels like a stork. I looked down at myself; the material was quite shiny which was an odd look for me. I did not look in the mirror this time; I knew I would look like neither myself nor like Pauline and it was too unsettling a prospect. I left off considering any jewellery or make-up, not wishing to be a figure of fun even for one evening. The dress was shiny enough without extra bling, and I didn't have any make-up anyway.

I don't know what it was. All evening I had the feeling that people were looking at me oddly, adjusting their features very consciously. Not the kids – the girls registered that I was dressed up and that was good enough for them. No, some of the staff, who saw me every day, seemed distant somehow, as if they didn't know what to say to me, reminding me of Jojo who could register the similarity between Pauline and me but couldn't work out why she wasn't there and I was. Maybe it was the cardigan. It was just an ordinary fleece cardigan that I used to wear for school. It had seen better days, I admit that. It was black and baggy but it felt to me a comforting thing, given that the dress was so far off what I was used to wearing. I knew it wasn't really the right thing, but I would need something if I was to be monitoring those chilly toilets or standing outside with the school mobile summoning some parent to come and take a child home because they were ill, or drunk, or hysterical, or generally out of order.

Apart from that little glitch it all was as I thought it would be. Outside the venue there was a bunch of parents taking photographs of their offspring as they appeared from out of their limousines in their finery and posed as if it was the Oscars. Some of the parents were people I had taught and I had to stop and try to remember their names and try to say something that was both pleasant and believable. One or two of them mentioned Pauline, but she had not taught there as long as I had and they knew her only as the other Miss Dearly who was so well-liked by their sons and daughters. Such a nice lady. Et cetera.

Next morning I passed the head's room on my way into school. Her door was open, as it always is, and she called to me to come in for a moment. I like her, Caroline, always have.

'All right Pam?' she said.

'Not bad,' I said.

'Prom went OK? For you I mean?'

'Same as always I suppose.'

She hesitated, which was unusual for her. 'Did I recognise Pauline's frock – the one you were wearing? I thought it was a nice touch.'

'Had to wear something.'

She got up from behind her desk and closed the door.

'Sit down for a minute,' she said. But I recognised the signs and told her that I had no time at the moment. I smiled at her so that she would know I was all right and got away. I did not know why she had called me in. I hadn't been drunk, I knew that. I'd had a drink or two but you know, it was a school do, there were kids there, it would not be professional to be drunk.

I unlocked my classroom. My form group – 11PD – would not be coming in today, nor ever again as a body. Small groups of them would dribble in for revision sessions in this or that subject and later for exams. They would come in August to get their GCSE results and later most of them would turn up for what we no longer called Speech Day, to receive their certificates. By then they would be unrecognisable – taller and well-groomed, swaggering shyly with grown-up-ness. I'd known this lot of kids for five years, ever since their first visit from their junior schools, before they had their uniforms, all nerves and watchfulness, all their top-of-the-school cockiness gone. Over the years there had been changes of personnel of course, people move away, one changed class for some now-forgotten reason, new ones arrived, but there they had all been, 11PD, cocky once again by being almost-leaving, nervous again at the thought of exams and sixth form college, or even going to work. I knew them, as much as a teacher can know them, from Amy to Zak, from Alvin to Vanessa; they were mine. Sometimes I looked at them as if they were all that I had left, and then I would think that in a few weeks they would be gone and what would I have then. I was missing them already. And I knew that I would have a new form – there would be 7PD to come back to after the summer, and knowing that made me realise how deeply, deeply I didn't want 7PD. I could not invest another five years, and all for nothing.

I tidied things up a bit and got out the materials for my first lesson. I didn't feel too great but I knew I would be feeling better than some of the younger staff who had not been so professionally careful about how much they had drunk. I taught my lesson, and then another one. I stayed in my room during break, wanting a cup of coffee but unable to face the staff room and wondering what it was about today that was making me feel lower than usual. After break I would be free so I would go then and get myself a hot drink. The staffroom by then would be full of dirty mugs but it would be quiet.

Walking along the corridor with my mug I met Frank Midgeley. Of the hundred or so staff members who were in our school, my favourite was Frank. He and I had been friends, in a work sense, for more years than we cared to count. I'd even known him at college, though he was two years above me and probably never noticed me. He wasn't that noticeable himself, except for his wild girlfriend – sooty eyes behind rainbow-dyed hair, dancing on her own, hair and arms going like machinery. She was training on the primary course but I gathered – though it wasn't something Frank and I ever discussed – that she failed her probationary year and then gave up. He was a geographer and had once been my Head of Department, in the days when we did Integrated Humanities, before he was elevated to Assistant Head. He was holding in his hand a pink slip of paper that meant he was on his way to remove a pupil from their class but he stopped to speak to me.

'All right?'

Of course I was. Or of course I wasn't. There seemed no difference to me in being all right or any other state.

'I'm fine,' I said. 'Thank you.' And again got away before he started saying something I had no intention of hearing.

But a few minutes later he appeared in my classroom.

'You should go home,' he said. 'You can't be in a fit state to work. Not after the evening you had.'

'What are you talking about?' I said. I truly had no memory of the evening I'd had.

He pulled a blue plastic chair away from its place and sat on it next to my desk. His creased jowly face seemed much too close but I believed he meant to be kind.

'All those tears,' he said. 'You must have been exhausted.'

'I don't know what you're talking about,' I said, and I truly didn't.

'After the prom,' he said, 'when we sat down for a drink. After all the kids had gone. Tears. I've never seen so many tears.'

I recalled, now, that extra drink, a few of us sitting at a table near the bar while staff cleared the room of the debris of what a hundred and fifty teenagers can do to a buffet. I recalled downing a large red wine. I did not recall crying in front of my colleagues. I would not have dreamt about doing such a thing. I remembered without warning that Barbara had said to me one evening as we were drinking gin and tonic, she said, 'Don't go getting upset now.' And Maureen had said, 'Never mind Bar, she can't help it can she.' I had not known what they were talking about.

'Did anyone notice?' I said, after some thought.

Frank appeared to think as well, and then said, 'I wouldn't worry about that. People understand.'

I doubted that. 'I'm all right,' I said. 'It's just a drop of alcohol that does it.'

'Sure,' he said. The bell went for the next lesson. 'You look after yourself now,' he said.

When I got home I picked Pauline's green dress up off the floor where I had dropped it the night before, intending, belatedly I know, to put it away. I didn't really know how to treat fancy clothes but thought maybe I should hang it up first for a bit, to let the creases sort themselves out.

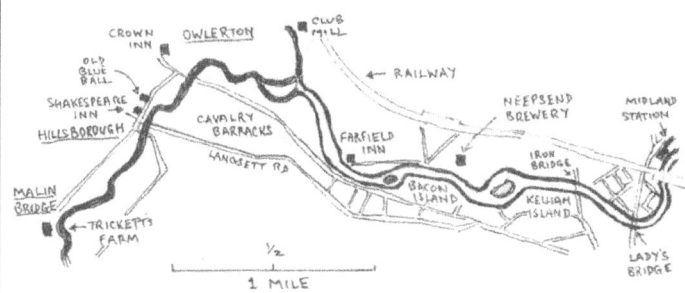

Malin Bridge to Owlerton

CSE Local History
Dale Dyke Dam Disaster
Worksheet 5

Write a story for a newspaper about the disaster. Include as many facts as you can and also some human interest stories.

N.B. This should be <u>at least</u> 300 words long.

You could shop in Hillsborough every day of your life and be completely unaware of the River Loxley, a quiet brown river running between shops and houses, shaded from sunlight and bordered by spindly trees and ramping brambles. It runs under the dual carriageway just by B & Q and gets lost behind factories until you find it again just before it turns east towards the city.

This was the hamlet of Owlerton, that now has no houses, only factories and yards, the dog track and the casino, and the new tertiary college. Back in 1864 it consisted of a number of houses, poor things mostly, and the flood raced through the streets, damaging houses, though having reached flatter ground some of the force had gone out of it. Enough though still to rip off gable ends and flood the downstairs and cellars of many. There were some good stories for the kids – the man who had been locked up in the police station for trying to kill himself by throwing himself in the river, but who decided, as the water rose higher in his cell, that he would prefer to live and shouted to be let out. It's the oddities that stick with you, as the newspapers have always known.

I never brought kids here though. The first few miles were the dramatic bit, and sufficed for a double lesson and the trip there and back in the minibus. Which I was allowed to drive in those days without taking any sort of test – just me, a battered minibus with no seat belts and a spur-of-the-moment decision to get out of school for an hour. No risk assessments either back then, no parental consent asked for. All in the past, like the cane and the slipper, fountain pens and free school milk. History.

I wandered around looking for the point where the Loxley meets the River Don, but I was unaccountably tired and found that I did not care enough to continue.

I couldn't see, from this point on, how to make it into a country walk that was either interesting or pleasant. All there was from now on was a river, sometimes accessible and more often not, bordered by factories and tyre fitters and spoiled with litter. I had not heard from Terry, not a squeak. He had forgotten all about it, I thought, it had been only something he'd thought up as a distraction for me, or else someone else had taken it on, someone more committed, who would put more energy into it and not be sidetracked by whatever it was that was hindering me.

It was the summer term. We were on the home straight now, we all said at school. It was May, the leaves were green, our Year Tens, like Jarvis, were getting ready for their work experience; the Year Elevens' exams were starting already even before the Spring Bank holiday. The dark evenings and the dark mornings were well in the past, there was a feeling, whether management liked it or not, of coasting to the finish line.

I smoked my Friday extra cigarette in my garden as the sun went down behind the Derbyshire hills and the sky turned pink. I could hear the plants growing, all the faint movements as they stretched and folded and settled for the night. I decided it was now safe enough from frost that I could plant courgettes in a pot or two, even though Pauline would not be there to cook them for me in the way I like but have never bothered to learn. I felt a little sad then, but it passed. I went to bed and slept well.

Next morning I woke up early, still feeling calm and peaceful. I thought to myself, in words, I'm over the worst, I thought.

I opened the curtains, the sun shone on the garden, still low, casting shadows and I saw that a tulip – the weather had made everything late that year – a tulip which the evening before had been still a bud, was now a proper flower, open and new, and all at once everything came back to me, crashing down on me, darkening everything, blinding me even, so that there was no sun, no flowers, no promise. I sat on the bed, I thought, this will pass, and it did – the first assault passed but there was no peace, no acceptance to follow.

I was a mechanical being again, dull and heavy like metal, slow and incapacitated, no good to myself or anyone, too shut down even to be angry. I went through the day, eating too much, drinking gin at lunch time and feeling worse, ignoring the phone when it rang and kicking the post, unopened, into a corner of the hall as I used to do at first.

In the afternoon the day clouded over and it turned colder and looked as if it would rain. I went out then, just as I was in my slippers and pyjamas with a thin jumper on top. I went along the edge and up to the woods. The birds were not even chirping now that the rain was falling and there was hardly anyone about – only a dog walker or two. I walked about there until I was wet through and the woods were getting dark. Pauline always said she did not like to walk her dog there when it was getting dark. It was a good place for a murderer, she thought. I would have welcomed a murderer.

At last when it was quite dark, I turned home. I decided I would drink all the drink I could find in the house and maybe die. But I wondered how I was going to get in to the house because I no longer had my door key. I had no pockets; I must have dropped it somewhere; I was not sure if I cared or not. Let me sit in the garden then, and die that way. But my front door was not even locked; the key was there, in the lock, on the outside for anyone to see. If there's a burglar inside, I thought, I'll just let him go. But there was no one inside. I had no desire to drink. I smoked a cigarette, ate a slice of dry bread, smoked another fag and then went to bed. I slept.

Jarvis was waiting for me after school again.

'It's the baby's birthday,' he said. 'Saturday. You could come.'

The baby's name was Jayden but so far no one used it. He was referred to only as 'the baby' and addressed variously as Pumpkin or Cuddles, or Nuisance, depending on circumstance.

'Did your mum send you?' I said.

'Sort of,' he said.

I did not ask what he meant – probably Heidi wanted me to keep Jojo out of the way while there was some kind of party; and she would think I should buy a present to add to the technicoloured heaps that littered the household.

'I'm sorry,' I said, though I wasn't. 'I'm busy on Saturday.'

He looked at me as if he didn't believe me but he didn't argue.

'Are you all right?' I said, because it struck me suddenly that he looked unhappy, pink around the nose, and he hadn't smiled once.

'Not bad,' he said.

'School OK?'

He twitched his face in an expression I took to mean, No worse than usual, and took a biscuit from the packet.

'Did you get your work experience sorted?'

He twitched again. 'I couldn't do the one I wanted. Someone else got it.'

'So what are you doing?'

'Got to go to the nursery.'

'Plant nursery? Or children?'

'Children,' he said. 'I might as well stay at home. It's the one where Cassie goes.'

'It's only two weeks out of your life,' I said. 'You'll be fine.'

'There's someone else going there too,' he said. 'A girl.'

'So you'll have someone to talk to, someone you know.'

He shrugged gloomily. 'She's not in my form. She probably won't even speak to me.'

'When do you start?'

'Monday.'

'Look,' I said. 'Everyone has to do it. You'll get something out of it. You'll learn something.'

'In my opinion,' he said, 'I know as much as I need to about childcare.'

I thought he was probably right.

'Everybody OK?' I asked, out of duty.

'Mum's got a new boyfriend,' he said.

'What's he like?'

He shrugged. 'All right. Better than Gavin anyway.'

He finished his mug of tea and began fidgeting as a precursor to actually going. 'So you won't be coming for the baby's birthday?'

'No,' I said. 'Tell your mum –' I couldn't think what he could tell her '– I'm going out Saturday.'

'With your boyfriend?' he said.

When I looked at his face I could see it was a joke; I laughed and he laughed too, a little, and then said, thoughtfully, 'You don't have boyfriends do you.'

'Not like your mum,' I said.

'Not like Granma,' he said. 'She had boyfriends didn't she?'

Did she?

'Did she?' I said.

When he was gone I thought about it. If Pauline had boyfriends I never knew about them, at least not in the years since Heidi left home. It should not have surprised me that Pauline went on having brief – or maybe not so brief – relationships with men. She scrubbed up well, as they say; she was friendly, occasionally flirtatious, she liked to go out for nice meals, she would dance if the opportunity arose. I supposed that sex must have been involved; even up to the time of her death perhaps. I thought back to her funeral – there were a few men there who I hadn't known but I assumed they were colleagues from one school or another. Now I wondered how many of them counted themselves as old boyfriends.

There had been a time – the few years between Heidi being about twelve and her first pregnancy – when she, Heidi I mean – would appear on my doorstep like Jarvis did now to complain about some new bloke who was hanging around her mother, or who had actually moved in. Sometimes, if he was particularly unlikeable Heidi would move in with me for a week or two. I used to moan about her being there, disrupting my life and having her friends in before I got home from work and using up all the bread and coffee, but I always knew she would go home again, when she could be sure once more of being the centre of her mother's attention. Although when she had gone I always felt a little bereft and my house seemed colder, and bleak for a few days until I adjusted. It was rather strange to think there had once been a time when you could have called us close.

'Is Jarv with you?

It was Heidi on the phone.

'Of course not,' I said.

'He hasn't come home.'

It was past ten o'clock, an inch off being properly dark. I knew it was the second week of his work experience; I hadn't seen him and if I thought anything at all I would have imagined it must have been going well.

'I haven't seen him,' I said. 'Have you tried his friends?'

'Of course I have,' she said crossly. I could hear her thinking, Did I think I was going to be the first person she contacted. 'Nobody's seen him.'

'What about that girl at the nursery? The one from his school. Do you know her name?'

'Alice,' she said. 'But they won't tell me where she lives, not even her phone number. They say it's private, they can't give it out without her permission.'

'They?'

'The nursery. Do you know what? He never turned up for work today and they never let me know. How irresponsible is that? I had to hear it from Cassie when she came home.'

'Thing is,' I said, 'he might have told them beforehand that he wasn't coming in. He could say – you know – he had a dentist's appointment, something like that.' You should know, I thought, you did enough of it when you were at school, telling lies and making excuses, writing your own absence notes and hiding the letters when they wrote to your mother.

'I thought he might be with you Pam.' Her voice had gone small as if she had realised that her last hope of an easy solution had gone. 'Are you sure he's not in your garden or somewhere?'

'He's not,' I said. 'I've been out there. I would have seen him.'

'Would you mind looking again?' I had never heard her so polite, and I opened the back door and walked around with the phone to my ear, and called his name a couple of times. At her end I heard a door open and she spoke to someone else. I guessed straightaway it was her new bloke and that he'd been sent out to look for the boy.

'Any luck?' I said.

'No,' she said.

'He'll be back,' I said. 'Where can he go after all? Let me know how things are in the morning.'

'All right,' she said, subdued, and put the phone down.

I had half-expected he might have come round to see me to tell me how it was going, the work experience, but I knew it was a lot to ask of a teenager. It seemed now as if he hadn't been enjoying it, and that was normal too. I wasn't really worried, myself. Jarvis had never had a taste of independence before; he'd always been kept close to his mum, and to Jojo, first off because he was a small child, and more recently because she needed him to help with the others. I could imagine how this had come about: he had dragged himself through one week of boring work, had a weekend and when Monday came around wouldn't have felt like starting another boring week. He would have wandered round a bit, maybe fallen in with some other truanting kids, and then been scared to go home and face his mum.

It was an hour later and I was just getting ready for bed when she rang again.

'I've notified the police,' she said. 'They say they'll look out for him.' She didn't allow me space to say anything.

I went back into my bathroom where the toothpaste was waiting on my brush. I opened the window and looked over the gardens and the one roof that lay between me and Pauline's bungalow. Once again I put off cleaning my teeth and went out of my house and round to the next street.

I let myself in through the back door. I switched on the kitchen light and went through into the sitting room. I did not know what I expected – Jarvis curled up on the settee, him and a mate playing cards – though anything like that would be out of character.

'Jarvis,' I called, in the voice that indicates that immediate obedience is in order, and then again, softer, 'Jarv? Are you here?'

He wasn't there and it seemed ridiculous to think that he might have been. I opened the bedroom doors and saw nothing. I wondered whether to let Heidi know and decided not to. There was nothing to tell. And yet, there was a different feel to the place, not a smell, not something out of place, just something. Stupid, I said to myself, wishful thinking. Remember all the prospective buyers and estate agents and surveyors who've been traipsing round here. If there's a presence it can only be theirs.

When I got home the landline was blinking with a message; I called Heidi back after all.

'Is he back?' I said. Although I was trying to dismiss any anxiety I was beginning to feel it a little.

'Pam, I've got these people here,' she said. 'Alice's parents. She's been missing all weekend.'

'I've just been round to the bungalow,' I said. 'Nobody's there.' I hadn't quite taken in what she had said, and as I realised I added, 'But they can't be together, surely. He said he hardly knew her.'

'They've been together for a week,' Heidi pointed out and I realised that that was long enough.

'But Jarv has been at home all weekend,' I said.

'He's come home to sleep,' she said. 'He's been out from early morning to his curfew. He told me he was round at Dom's house, but Dom says – and Dom's mum says – he's not been there at all.'

I could not think what to say, or do.

'Can you come round,' she said. 'Please Pam.'

I waited for her to say sorry but she didn't and then I thought of Jarvis and realised I wanted to know very much that he was all right.

'I can't bear,' she said, 'for something else . . .' and I thought, No I can't either.

'Ten minutes,' I said.

Cassie and the baby were in bed of course, but Jojo was sitting in his usual place, looking from face to face as if confused but at moments distracted by the television which was silently on. The new boyfriend, whose name was Adam, was offering to make tea and coffee, unheard because the other man in the room – presumably the father of Alice – did not stop talking.

'Tell me from the beginning,' I said.

Alice's mother looked ready to drop from tiredness; she took a mug of tea from Adam's hand and I was afraid she would let it fall, just from forgetting to hold it.

There had been a bit of a row, I gathered, last Thursday evening. 'Nothing unusual,' said the father, 'just a bit of a bust up with her sister, it happens all the time. Sent them both to their rooms to calm down, Alice is screaming down the stairs that she hates us all and she's going to run away.'

'Has she run off before?' I asked.

'No,' he said, and the mother corrected him. 'She's said it before. She's been missing for an hour or two, sort of cooling off, you know. She's never stayed out overnight before –' She bent her head over her mug of tea and tears dropped into it.

'But she went off OK on Friday morning,' said the dad. 'I dropped her off, she was a bit sullen, but nothing unusual.'

'She was there all day,' said the mum. 'She just never came home.'

Of course they had been to her friends, to her grandparents in Chesterfield and in High Green. They had driven around, and walked around, and shown her photo to people, and asked everyone they could think of to search for her. And of course the police were involved, and keeping their eyes open and calling at places where teenagers were known to gather.

She was nothing to do with me but even so I felt the escalating possibilities run through my mind – boyfriend, bus to another city, scared to come back; hiding in some house nearby, drugs and alcohol; abuse and overdoses and rape and murder; never being seen alive again.

'Three nights,' Heidi told me. 'Friday, Saturday, Sunday she's been gone, and now Monday.'

'But Jarvis came home?' I said.

'But today neither of them turned up at their placement,' said Adam. 'And he's not come home.'

It was midnight. Heidi suddenly remembered Jojo and packed him off to bed. I remembered that I had to get up for work the next morning but it seemed rude to leave them in their helpless misery.

'I went to the bungalow,' I said. 'But there was no sign that anyone had been there.'

'I already looked,' said Heidi. 'That was just before I called you the first time.'

'What it looks like to me,' I said, 'is that your daughter has been hiding somewhere all weekend and I bet Jarvis has been aware of where she was, and today he's been with her too. Which in a way is a good thing. They must be safer together.' No one appeared to be cheered up though.

We sat. Alice's mother checked something called a Facebook page. The father called the police again to ask if there was any news.

'We should be at home,' said the woman. 'My parents are there,' she explained to me, 'with our other daughter, but if there's any news I want to be at home.'

That was a relief to me and I could see from Heidi's face that she felt it too.

But when they had gone it seemed to make things worse. Adam, apologising, said he had to go home to bed, and went. So he hadn't turned into a live-in boyfriend yet. I wanted more than anything to go home too but Heidi said, 'Don't go Pam.'

I so wanted to go home to my own bed, but she had it all worked out.

'Sleep in my bed,' she said. 'I'll stay down here, for when he comes home. In case he comes home. But I might need to go and fetch him from somewhere – if he phones. If the police phone. I need someone here. You'll get to sleep, the kids are all in bed. I wouldn't ask, Pam –' she's one of those who uses your name a lot '– but you can see I've got no one else.'

She didn't say, Now, but I knew she thought it. I knew she was saying it to make me stay, *and* I knew she truly did need someone there.

So I stayed. She lay down on the settee, clutching her phone in her hand and I went and lay on her bed, just as I was, in my clothes. Sleep seemed a long way off. I thought about Jarv, in different scenarios, each worse than the one before. I thought about drugs, and knives, and punishments, about rapists and trafficking gangs. I imagined a story where he and Alice had made a suicide pact and gone and jumped off a bridge over the M1. I considered that she, Alice herself, might be murderously inclined. I knew – of course I knew – that teenagers go missing all the time, and that most of them turn up, sheepish and hungry and with the lesson learned; but there are those that don't. There are accidents and crimes awaiting some of them, and misjudgements, and plans that go wrong. Some of those sulky, stroppy kids – not that Jarv was like that – some of them only turn up as dead bodies. It did not bear thinking about, I could not bear thinking about it, but I couldn't stop thinking. Pauline, I thought to myself, would never get over it.

When I heard the phone I woke out of a sleep that seemed to have been too short. A little light was coming through the gap in the curtains. I shut my eyes to pretend I hadn't heard anything, but opened them again and went downstairs. She was sitting up, the phone still pressed to her ear, and tears were running down her face.

'Thank you,' she said into the phone, and switched it off.

I waited, though I could tell from her face that he was all right.

'They found him,' she said. 'Doncaster. Hiding behind the recycling bins, both of them. They're on their way back with them. They told Alice's parents first, I guess cos she's been gone for longer.'

'Did you speak to him?'

'They said they were asleep in the back of the police car.'

'I suppose,' I said, 'you don't get a lot of sleep behind a recycling bin.'

'He called the police himself,' she said. 'Jarvis did, on her phone. He called 999 and told them they were lost and people were threatening them and they were hiding, and he told them which supermarket to find them.'

'I'll be off home then,' I said. 'I need to get dressed for school and get myself together. You'll be all right now.'

'You don't want to stay and see him?' she said.

'I'll see him soon enough,' I said. 'Don't be too hard on him will you – I bet it was that Alice's idea and you know what a soft touch he is. He only wants to help, you know that.'

'I won't kill him,' she said.

At the door – daylight now – she smiled at me. 'I couldn't have – I couldn't have coped if something happened to him,' she said. 'Ever since – you know – since Mum died I'm scared something else will happen. I can't stop thinking about what could happen.'

'You're not being logical,' I said, and she nodded, and shrugged, and I knew I was no more logical than she was, and I went home and started on another day.

My Year Tens, due to start their own work experience the week after the Spring Bank holiday, were buzzing with the story of Alice, her disappearance and her recovery. Not surprising – she and Jarvis attended their school less than a mile away from ours and some of my girls knew her personally and were able to put others right when they got her name wrong. Was she Alice or Alicia or Alisha? Was she Alisha Wood or Alice Sherwood? Word of mouth had warped her proper name out of her. She was weird anyway, I was informed. So far, Jarvis' name had not been made public and there was speculation as to who would be insane enough to get tangled up with Alice. 'She's a nutter.'

I was not to see Jarvis until the Friday. Heidi made sure that he went off to his work placement; being chased round central Doncaster by drug dealers was not going to get him any concessions. He was allowed a shower, and breakfast and then, not even very much later than he should have been, he was escorted by her to the Supertots nursery where the manager promised to be in immediate contact if he so much as went out of the front door. He arrived home, bringing Cassie with him, at the proper time, ate a large bowl of pasta and went to bed. Heidi told me all this on the phone that evening, sounding, herself, quite recovered from the event.

'We were right,' she said. 'Alice *was* at the bungalow. Three nights, Friday, Saturday, Sunday. Then Jarv got scared that people might come round to look at it – he never seemed to think we might call in there, or that people look at houses at a weekend – so they went down to town and just got on a random bus and hung around Doncaster. Then got scared of the people they were seeing around them.'

'He's OK?' I said.

'A bit subdued,' she said. 'I think he's found out that Alice is trouble. I hope he manages to keep away from her when they go back to school.'

'Did she go to the nursery today?'

'Her parents are keeping her at home. Her mother called me, not happy with Jarv obviously, but *really* bothered about Alice. I got the impression they're hauling her off to a psychiatrist.'

'And how are you?' I said, remembering my manners.

'I'm all right,' she said. 'Littlest one has been crabby all day – back teeth I think; I'm hoping for an early night. And I want to say thanks Pam, for coming round. I know we –'

'I know,' I said. 'We don't need to go over that. Tell Jarvis I want to see him at the weekend.'

'All right,' she said. 'Bye then.' I heard a tiny breath of something then; it might have been a Sorry.

'I'm sorry too,' I said softly, but it was probably too late.

Of course when he came, on Friday evening, with Jojo, he was as calm and unanimated as ever. I wondered – I had wondered before – if he ever laughed out loud.

'Well,' I said. 'What did you learn from all that?'

'Don't run away again,' he said in a silly voice.

'Seriously,' I said. 'I know there was no harm done, in the end, but –'

'I know,' he said. '*You* don't have to tell me as well. I know.'

'Is Alice your girlfriend?'

He looked horrified. 'Nobody wants her for a girlfriend,' he said. 'Not even a friend. She's weird. She told me she would kill herself. She told me –' he looked down at his mug of chocolate '– I don't really want to tell anyone all the stuff she told me. I said I wouldn't. Not even mum.'

'Do you think she meant it?'

'Which bit?'

'I suppose, mainly about killing herself. If you know something like that you have to think, Do you need to tell someone? Think how awful it would be if she tried it, and we knew all the time and hadn't told her parents.'

He wouldn't say any more, but I hoped he would give it some thought. I had come across those suicidal teenage girls myself but luckily – for me and for them – it wasn't my job to have a great deal of sympathy for them. Other people were employed to have them weeping in their offices, and to make excuses for their bad behaviour, lack of coursework, poor attendance, all that sort of thing. I had had enough of all that when Heidi was young and if I was no good at it for my own niece I couldn't see that I should try helping someone else's child.

Since Pauline died the idea of killing myself had of course come into my mind. Sometimes it just passed through, a small speculative notion that I could more or less ignore; sometimes I summoned it on purpose and gave it serious thought. Why shouldn't I, what was there to stop me? I could do whisky and paracetamol – who would notice, who would care? It shouldn't be painful. I could leave a note in school on a Friday – for Frank probably – so that he would find it Monday morning, I could do the deed Sunday evening and I shouldn't smell too badly by the time they came to the house. It's what they call, I believe, having a Plan, and is a Bad Sign, but I was too cowardly to try it. If I had believed in an afterlife, or in being reunited, that might have swung it, but as it was, then no.

I thought again about the man in 1864 who wanted to kill himself and then decided it was not such a good idea after all to die. I looked him up in my book to see if his name had been recorded, and found that the story was even more loaded with dramatic irony. He was released from his cell, by now four feet deep in water by the police inspector, who, poor man, caught typhus and died two months later. Just goes to show – you can't tell what your actions are going to set off. I did not want to be a trouble to anyone; I did not want to change my mind and start ringing for an ambulance and end up having my stomach pumped, or whatever they do to you now, alongside a bunch of sad cases who had, like me, overdosed and then regretted it. I did not want the embarrassment so I stayed alive – half alive – to avoid it.

My spring bank holiday week was, I suppose, quiet. Heidi called me to say that Adam was taking the week off and that they were going to take the children out for days. She didn't actually ask if I wanted to go with them but I could tell that if I had wanted to I could have.

'Also,' she said, 'I'm thinking about where would be a good place to scatter mum's ashes.

I said nothing.

'I mean, all right,' she said, 'I don't want to keep a jar of ashes and neither do you but you're supposed to scatter them somewhere significant aren't you?'

I still said nothing. I could not think of anything to say. I wanted to put the phone down and get back into bed with my head under the covers.

'I'm right though aren't I? Somewhere nice as well, so that you can go there and remember her and all that. Which I would like to do, but I don't know anywhere that she especially liked to go to. Do you?'

Well, I didn't. If it had been me there'd have been no problem – anywhere in Derbyshire would do, up a hill preferably, Stanage Edge or Mam Tor. My ashes would blow in a thousand bits in all directions and never come together again. I could think of any number of high and wild places, but not a single one that could conceivably be connected with Pauline. The places she liked were places like Meadowhall and Fargate. If we could sprinkle her from the café floor of John Lewis she would be happy, but I did not say so.

Heidi gave up on me and changed the subject. She said she'd received a decent offer for the bungalow and accepted it. Of all things, the people had looked at it on the Friday, only hours before Alice took up her place hiding in the attic there, and made a second visit on the Monday, soon after she and Jarvis had decamped.

'Asking price?' I said.

'No more, no less,' she said. 'Retired I think, downsizing probably. I haven't met them. Don't want to anyway.'

'We'll have to get the furniture moved out before they move in.'

'Not this week,' she said. 'Not with all the kids at home. Unless –' she paused. I could hear her thinking. '– you'd be willing to see to it.'

Well, I had nothing else to do.

The weather was fine that week. I could have – in fact I had planned to – walk from Hillsborough into the city as close as I could to the river, passing the site of the Sheffield workhouse. This was severely flooded back then in 1864 but no lives were lost and the building was used, along with several public houses, as a place to bring dead bodies to be identified. I might still do it, I thought, but I'll get clearing the bungalow out of the way first. I had been able to consult with Heidi about what to sell and what to keep for her, and with her permission I took photographs and went home to my computer to offer the furniture for sale to the highest bidder who would come and carry them away.

Pauline had quite a flamboyant taste in furniture as well as in clothes. Her sofas were more striking than comfortable; her dining table and chairs were more suited to a minor stately home than to a 1970s bungalow. Her curtains were heavy with lining and finished off with pelmets and tie-backs. The rooms were busy even without her extensive collections of ornamental pigs and owls, and fake art-deco bronzes, and quirky table lamps which I had taken home and were now cluttering my smallest bedroom, with an overflow on to the landing. I told her once it was like a tart's boudoir and she laughed and told me I knew nothing about home décor or tarts, and neither of us took offence. That's how it was, nearly always; We could say what We liked to each other and it was never – almost never – a cause for a quarrel.

I spent some time in her garden, starting by going through her shed and wondering whether there were any tools I should take, but I couldn't come to any decision and I then allowed myself to be sidetracked into tidying up her flower beds. Not that there was much in them. Of course none of her usual bedding plants had been put in that spring. I pulled up the weeds and purloined the last of her pots, by now containing only dead things. I took them home to my garden just as they were, never one to waste good composting material. I considered buying in some petunias to brighten up the back of the house but decided against it. The new people might not move in until the autumn; petunias would be shrivelled and dry by then.

I went there every day that week, usually to wait for someone with a van who had bought furniture. The oak table and high-back chairs, that looked like something out of a medieval soap opera, were taken away by a wannabe footballer's wife type who needed something big to fill her new house. The chaise longue went to an elderly couple who had just had a new conservatory built on to their same-as-mine-and-three-million-others semi. The wardrobes were all built in; the washing machine I practically gave away to a young couple and Heidi was having the twin beds. No takers for the king-size double – what did she need that for, my sister, who slept on her own. Didn't she? At the end of the week a housing charity came and took it away.

Everything that went left a cleaning job behind. Her hoover was way better than mine and I knew I would take it for myself after I had dealt with the accumulated dust from under these heavy chairs and things that no one, not even my house-proud sister would move every week.

And by Friday I was finding it quite hard to have any emotion whatsoever.

Going back to school really did feel like the last lap now. Every morning I hovered outside the Sports Hall while the Year Elevens arrived, agitated or nonchalant according to the act of the day. One day as they came out of their last Maths exam, I pulled Daisy to one side and asked her how she was, and how her stepfather was getting on.

'Your mum told me,' I said, 'that he was waiting for surgery.'

'He's had it,' she said. 'He's back home now.'

'Did it go all right?'

'I suppose so,' she said. 'He has to take tablets though.'

'Exams going all right?' I said.

She shrugged. 'It'll be all right when they're over.'

'Daisy.' She was not in the least like Heidi had been; there was not a bit of defiance in her, only a sort of hopelessness. 'Daisy, what's the matter?'

We were standing near the office area; I opened the door to the little room where sick children wait to be taken home – it was empty.

'Daisy, you've done all the right things. You've applied to college, you've done your revision, you've nearly got to the end of your exams. Your mum must be really proud the way you've turned it round. *I'm* really proud of you.'

She shrugged again. 'There's no point though, is there?'

'In what way, no point?'

'What's it all for?' she said.

That stumped me. Around us I could hear the voices of children being let out of school for lunch break; I could hear telephones ringing in the office; I could feel the whole edifice of the school sheltering us and giving a semblance of meaning to my life.

'I don't know,' I said. 'You'll have to ask someone cleverer than me. But it'll be all right. Don't worry. Whatever it is, it will be all right in the end.'

Fool, I thought as I watched her walk out of the gate and across to the sandwich shop. It was not Daisy who I thought was a fool.

The Year Tens were all out of school learning about sweeping the floors of hairdressers or holding a ladder while someone else did something slightly more interesting at the top of it. Though there were six weeks still to go until the end of term they would be punctuated by sports days and trips out and at the back of all our minds there would be the prospect of setting the children to some undemanding task – probably involving colouring – that would keep them amiably occupied while we emptied our cupboards and filled our paper recycling bags with redundant memos and directives and plans and suggested improvements and reminders and conduct reports and minutes of meetings and urgent requests for decisions and lost exercise books and someone's missing project.

Also there were visits to our pupils out on work experience. I guess most of us teachers relished getting out of the confines of school, on a pleasant summer day, driving without particular hurry to some establishment or other, chatting to a supervisor, asking a few questions of the kid and driving back to school the long way round, marvelling at how life goes on while we – kids and staff – are tucked away in classrooms, out of sight.

I manoeuvred to go and visit Supertots Nursery where Jarvis had been, just out of nosiness. Of course as I walked in I saw Cassie and she looked at me curiously, as if she wasn't sure who I was, and didn't come running to greet me as she would have done six months ago. Six months. It was even more than that by now.

'Pam Dearly,' I said. 'Come to visit Alexandra.'

The woman in charge – matron? manager? – did not seem to make any connection with my name and that of Cassie or Jarvis. She waved her hand at the corner where Alexandra, a dutiful girl, was reading a story to a small bunch of tots and any thought I had of having a conversation about Alice and Jarvis and the drama of the previous week disappeared. It would have been unprofessional anyhow, but if she had started it I would have had to go along with it, wouldn't I?

Of course there was no such thing as Work Experience when We were at school. Our sisters and brothers left school at fourteen or fifteen and started doing proper work, with clocking on and all the factory pranks of being sent to ask someone for a long stand or a left-handed screwdriver. But they had a pay packet at the end of the week. Auntie Vi was firmly opposed to us having a Saturday job, but We, seduced by the prospect of an extra pound a week, were desperate to work in one of the local shops.

'You need your rest of a weekend,' she said. 'You've got homework to do.' We used to plead with her and promise to do our homework on Friday nights.

'No you won't,' she said. 'You'll want to be out Friday nights. And Saturdays.' This was true; it was what We wanted the extra pound for. 'And then you'll be tired to death on Sunday and you won't get your homework done.'

'What if,' said Pauline. 'What if We had one job between us? I could do the morning and she could do the afternoon. Or the other way round.'

'Don't be ridiculous,' said Vi, and then ended it by saying, 'Your mother would never forgive me if I let you spoil your schoolwork.'

'She wouldn't mind,' We said. 'Maureen and Barbara never stayed on at school.'

'Times were different then,' said Vi. She walked back into the kitchen, throwing over her shoulder, 'You live with me, you do as I say.'

And there was no answer to that.

So until We did our first teaching practice We had no idea what it was like to spend the whole day on our feet, doing things wrong, getting our lesson plans mixed up – or not having them at all – having to learn who of the rest of the staff was who and what their particular quirks and skills might be. Who might be able to locate the lost set of text books for me, who might, for Pauline, be able to explain how the sewing machines could be made to function.

So the term dribbled away. The paper bins filled to overflowing. The sports day event was washed out by exceptional rainfall and had to be relocated to the Sports Hall, luckily not needed that day for exams.

'It's almost more tiring than proper teaching,' said Frank to me, as we ushered them off the premises and out into the still pouring rain well before the proper time. 'Year Six visits next week.'

These were the new children who would replace the Year Elevens. I groaned. 'I don't know if I can do it,' I said. I couldn't have said it to anyone but Frank. 'I don't have the – the wherewithal to start all over again. And they are so demanding. They fight and they cry, and their parents are always on the phone, and they want them moved into another form and they want them to have more homework, or less homework, and I have to patch up their friendships.'

'I know,' he said.

'Of course you know,' I said. 'Take no notice of me, I'm just having a moan. Just, give me Key Stage Four any day.'

'Actually,' he said, 'here's an idea. How about you taking over Pauline's form? They've been messed about this year with different form tutors, ever since – you know. They need someone who knows all about getting through Year Eleven.'

I wished I had thought of it. I didn't like to have someone else, not even Frank, solving a problem for me, but I wasn't about to be too sensitive. 'Can that be juggled?'

He briefly explained who would be moved, who wouldn't mind at all, how the head of year would be happy to have me. 'Leave it with me,' he said. 'I'll let you know on Monday, after the team meeting.'

'Thank you,' I said, and he patted me on the shoulder. 'Least I can do,' he said.

It rained all the next day too, though not quite as heavily, and when I got home that afternoon – end of another week, another weekend to be filled – I found my machine flashing with messages. Before I could even find who they were from the doorbell rang and before I got there to open it I saw Jojo walking in. Followed by Adam, and the two little children.

'Baby can walk now,' Cassie informed me.

Adam – a surprisingly nice young man – had seen the look on my face.

'They can't stay at home,' he said.

They can't stay here, I was about to say.

'We're flooded,' he said. 'I mean, Heidi's flooded.'

I imagined an overflowing washing machine, a puddle on the floor, a leaking radiator, Heidi making a drama of it.

'I need to get back,' said Adam. 'Here's their stuff. It's a bit random I'm afraid.'

Their stuff was in bin bags. I could hear that Jojo had turned the TV on.

'What about Jarvis?' I said. It was meant as sarcasm but he didn't notice. 'He's helping,' he said. 'It's a nightmare.'

172

'How long?' I said. The bin bags were quite full, and there was a whole bag of nappies besides.

'Can't tell. Look, got to get back. She'll ring you later.' He had not come in further than the doormat and now he backed out again. 'Nightmare,' he repeated.

I looked at the pile of belongings, at the two small children looking back at me, warily trusting. Nightmare seemed to be the word.

'What happened?' I said to Cassie.

'Water all over,' she said matter-of-fact-ly.

'Where from? Did the washing machine overflow?'

She looked puzzled.

'Where did the water come from?'

'From the garden,' she said. 'It came in through the door.' This made no sense to me, and I tried Heidi's phone, and then the landline, but there were no replies.

The baby had been sitting on the floor of my hall all this time, chewing on some toy or other but he suddenly seemed to realise that he was away from home, and away from his mother, and he threw the toy down and scrambled to his feet and began to totter about, starting to make moaning sounds that I felt would become more insistent.

'He wants juice,' said Cassie.

Well, I could manage that. I found a bag with food and drink in it, bottles and sippy cups, bibs and wetwipes. I gave him juice; I gave them all juice. It bought a few seconds of peace before the moaning started again.

'What does he want now?' I said.

Cassie suggested chocolate but I didn't want them being sick. We were still in the hall; Cassie was searching through the bags for some of her toys, beginning herself, now that the situation was sinking in, to be thinking of being tearful. I herded them into the sitting room and sat them in front of the TV. Jojo was watching something with people making robots

173

out of scrap; I had to promise Cassie Peppa Pig at the end of his programme. I thought about giving them food but wondered how we would get through the evening if I fed them too early. I wanted my cigarette and I also wanted a large alcoholic drink, not waiting till nine-thirty as I usually did.

'Done a poo,' Cassie said, waving her hand at the baby. I thought that if Jarvis had been there I would have persuaded him to do the necessary, but as he wasn't it came down to me. I bribed Cassie with a further promise of two episodes of Peppa Pig if she would come to the bathroom with me, to help. She wasn't about to touch anything I could tell, but she stood by the door, making disgusted noises and offering bits of advice, some of it helpful. 'Don't put it there –' it being the dirty one '– he'll try to get it.' 'Give him something to play with, else he'll roll over.' I gave him my nailbrush which went straight to his mouth. Pauline would have snatched it away but I let him keep it.

I emptied the binbags – my life seemed to consist of emptying binbags – so that I knew what equipment I had and didn't have. I was briefly grateful that the dog had been put down and I didn't have to have that as well. I made a plan to give them beans on toast as soon as they started to say they were hungry, or when Peppa Pig lost its appeal, whichever came sooner. I worked my self into a state of indignation that Heidi would so impose upon my Friday evening and planned that if she hadn't phoned by seven o'clock I was going to load them all in the car – car seats or no – and take them back home, because by then the clearing up would surely be finished.

While I was trying to feed the baby with mashed up baked beans, and at the same time reassure Jojo, who I could see was becoming worried, and at the same time stop Cassie from getting down before she'd even tried to eat anything – while all this was going on, and the noise of the television still from the other room – the doorbell rang and here was Adam again, this time carrying four or five shopping bags, the biggest sort.

'Good to see you,' I said. 'They'll be ready in no time at all.'

He looked at me. 'They can't come back,' he said, 'if that's what you're thinking. No way. Where's your freezer?'

Now I only had a fridge-freezer, nothing like as big as the chest freezers that Pauline and Heidi had and if he thought he was going to fit the contents of all those bags in it he had another think coming. But it was luckily not very full at all and he set to and managed to cram in an awful lot, and piled the rest in the fridge. 'Feel free to use it up,' he said.

'But what is going on?' I said to his back as he knelt wrestling a family tub of ice cream into a space that I thought it wouldn't go into.

'We're flooded,' he said eventually, closing the door with some difficulty.

'How?'

'Haven't you seen the news? We're all over it.'

'Burst pipes? What?'

He shrugged. 'Don't know yet, not really. Blocked drains in the street isn't helping but mostly it's the brook overflowing.'

'What that little brook? That can't make much of a flood.'

'Well it has.' He was being quite patient with me really. 'All this rain is just too much for it. Probably blocked as well, debris, you know, washed down. So it's over its banks and of course it's at the end of the garden, no distance at all.'

'So your cellar's flooded?' I was beginning to grasp it.

'Cellar's flooded, ground floor's flooded –'

'So the freezer –' Heidi's freezer was down in the cellar.

'And the washing machine.' That was in the cellar too and Heidi used it at least once every day.

'Electric's off. We've taken what we can upstairs, but downstairs – well, it's all ruined, you know, carpets, settees, lot.'

He went away and later Heidi turned up, without warning, in time to watch herself on the ten o'clock news. Jojo was still watching the telly, Cassie was asleep in one of the twin beds and I had hoped to put the baby in with her, wedged up against the wall so that he couldn't fall out, but he had screamed so that I had to bring him downstairs before he set Cassie off – she was being impressively brave actually – and he was now lying on my settee, taking up more room than a small child should be able to, arms and legs flung out, sleeping the sleep of the baffled and exhausted.

Heidi looked worn out too. I made her coffee and sandwiches and she told me Adam had stayed in the house, with Jarvis – she'd left them sitting upstairs, by candlelight, eating fish and chips.

'What else can happen?' she said. 'Honestly, I feel like – I feel like –' and she began to cry, noisily at first but then, seeing Jojo take notice and begin to crumple, she made herself go quiet and only the water running down her face showed.

'Can't even have a good cry,' she said, half laughing.

'I can't believe,' I said, 'that that little brook can cause so much damage.'

'I can,' she said vehemently. 'We've been telling them for months it was blocked. Environmental Health said it's Environment Agency's job, they say it's down to the council, they come and look and say not to worry. And now look at it.'

So it really was a big deal. Heidi's house was on a tucked away little street in Chapeltown, close to the park. Her mother had helped her with the deposit – I say helped, but I think she paid all of it – at the time when Jojo was a baby and his father Alasdair was still around, and employed enough to cover the monthly mortgage payments. A nice little terraced house, not the most convenient, with the bathroom downstairs and no hall to park a buggy in, but it was in a friendly street and she had pleasant neighbours – every one of them had also been flooded, as we saw on the local news, images of people with brooms trying to get the water out of their precious houses, and the water flowing back into the houses because there was nowhere else for it to go. I also realised that my whole weekend had gone. These children were not going home this side of Monday.

'You're going to need to stay aren't you,' I said.

She gave me a look. 'Obviously,' she said.

'It's all right,' I said. 'I just need to go and clear some space in the boxroom so Jojo can sleep on the floor in there. Then you can go in with Cassie.'

She didn't offer to help me, for which I was glad because seeing her mother's stuff dumped all over like the end of a car boot sale might have led to more tears, or else recriminations. I understood anyway that she was exhausted by bailing and sweeping and organising, and by the realisation of what she had to look forward to.

I shifted the stuff into my room, crammed into the bottom of the wardrobe, under the bed, piled under the window. As I closed the curtains I looked down over the gardens as I always did at the roof of Pauline's bungalow.

'Listen,' I said to Heidi, 'listen to this.'

'But there's no furniture there,' she said. 'It's under offer. I don't even have a key any more.'

'I do,' I said. 'You know there's no room here for all of you. There's nowhere for Jarvis, never mind Adam –'

'Adam doesn't live with me,' she said. Adam, though I hadn't known this, was married and still living with his wife, though she couldn't be seeing much of him.

'Even so. As I was saying – you haven't exchanged contracts, the place is still yours, you could use it for a few days, even just for sleeping. I can get some camp beds from school, or Adam could bring your mattresses over from home. You could even have your meals there. The cooker is still there isn't it. You'd all be together – after all, it might be a week or two before your house is liveable in.'

She looked at me again; her face seemed to have aged and sagged. 'A week or two,' she said. 'You don't know what you're talking about.'

I did not actually say the words, You can't all stay here, but I knew she heard them.

'There's only two bedrooms,' she said.

'There's only two here,' I said, 'that are spare.'

'The fridge is still there, right? And the cooker?'

'Built in,' I said.

'I don't know,' she said. 'I've got Jojo to get to school, and Cassie to get to nursery. I can hardly afford to run the car as it is. And what would Jojo be like, in *her* house? It would really confuse him. I wish we could go home.'

'You just said,' I said, 'you just said it would be weeks till you can get back in.'

'Months,' she said sadly. 'Adam thinks the floorboards will need replacing and the plaster may have to come off the walls. First thing tomorrow I've got to call the insurance.'

'You won't be the only one.'

'No,' she said. 'Whole street's completely fucked. Old people, everyone, and everyone's got too much to do to help anyone else. It's awful. We're lucky, having you here to pick up the pieces.'

That's a new role for me, I thought.

'Look,' I said. 'How about this? You and the little ones go and stay in the bungalow – not tonight, I don't mean that – and Jojo can stay here.'

Jojo was still watching TV with Violet the cat on his knee.

'I don't know,' said Heidi.

'Jarvis could stay here too,' I said, cunningly. 'They could share the bedroom, like they do at home.

178

Jojo would have a familiar face around.' Jarvis would help, was what I was thinking.

'I don't know,' she said again.

'Think it over,' I said. 'Another thing –' I could hardly believe I was saying this '– I could take Jojo and Cassie in the mornings if it would save you a trip.'

'What about the buyers?' she said.

'It's still your house,' I said. 'We can ask the estate agent – no, not ask, tell them no one can move in for – how long? A month, maybe.'

I was very wrong about that, as it turned out.

Maureen was overflowing with sympathy when I told her the news. 'Poor Heidi. I remember what it was like in '53, the smell and the mud and the damp. You thought it would never go away. Our dad was months getting the house sorted out and repaired. I think, if I remember rightly, that the boys got some leave and came home to help him.' She meant Jim and Eddie of course – Alan would have been too young to help, and Vincent was in hospital still.

Verona, phoning almost as soon as Maureen had got off the phone, offered to come up and help Heidi but I assured her that she could do nothing. 'It's all pumps and machinery,' I said. 'They've got driers in, and then it will be builders – you know, plasterers and electricians, that sort of thing.'

'You know,' she said, 'my parents left Canvey after the flood. My mum would have stayed but my dad said he wasn't going through that again; that's why they moved to Dagenham.'

I could dimly remember her parents, enough to be faintly pleased that her dad had got his own way on at least one thing in his life.

Of course Alan was not far behind with his phone call. 'Awful,' he said. 'Just awful. And without her mum there to support her.'

She's got me, I felt like saying.

'What would she have said, Pauline I mean. And all of us down here, too far away to do anything. I always say, if you can't depend on your family, then who can you depend on.'

I was happy to hear, at that point, a loud cry of something like anguish from the other room. 'Thanks for calling,' I said. 'Got to go. Busy.'

Heidi was standing looking out of the window and naturally I went and looked out too, but there seemed nothing to see. The boys were simultaneously watching TV and listening to music through headphones. There seemed to be nothing to shriek about. She beckoned me away from them into the kitchen and stood leaning against the fridge, beginning to cry, I thought, although she seemed to be laughing as well.

'What?' I said.

'Mum's ashes,' she said, choking with either laughter or tears. 'I forgot all about them.'

'What about them?'

'They were in our cellar, so –'

'What were they doing down there?'

'Being kept out of the reach of children,' she said sharply. 'Did you think I was going to let the babies play with them?'

'So?'

'The cellar's been cleared. Today. Adam got some people on to it.'

'What everything?'

'He made a list, for the insurance – he just texted me asking what the big heavy jar was. I'd forgotten it was there.'

How could she, I thought. *I* wouldn't have.

'So it's where now?'

'Taken to the council tip with everything else.'

'Didn't Adam realise what it was? When he made the list?'

'Well no. I'd never seen a jar of ashes before, so why should he?'

We had a bit of a silence then.

180

'At least –' she said.

'We don't have to scatter them –'

'One less thing to think about –'

Washed away, I was thinking, perished in the flood, like our mother.

'Have you been smoking?'

He shrugged. 'Maybe.'

'Jarv,' I said.

'*You* do,' he said.

'That,' I said, 'is exactly what makes me tell you *not* to. Do you know how much money it has cost me over the last forty-five years?'

'I'm not going to do it for forty-five years,' he said.

'Oh what? You're going to smoke for a week, get addicted and then give up?'

'I might.'

'Do you know how hard it is to give up? Do you know how hard it is for me to keep it down to two a day?'

'I've seen you smoke more than two,' he said.

'Because it's hard.'

'Adam smokes,' he said. 'Smokes weed too.'

'I bet your mum doesn't let him smoke in the house.'

'No she doesn't.'

'And there's a reason for that isn't there.'

'She doesn't like the smell?'

(Who could *not* like the smell, I thought.)

'*And* she doesn't want her children to get the idea that it's an OK thing to do. Get it? What do you think your Granma would have said?'

He shrugged some more.

'Look,' I said. 'I'm on your side Jarv, you know that. But if I smell fags on you – or weed, come to that – I'll tell your mum I promise you. I won't say anything this time, but if I ever find out again – or even suspect – I'm warning you, she'll know about it.'

He tried to look defiant but his face wasn't really made for it, and he took a biscuit from the packet instead.

'So hand over your fags,' I said.

He started to say he hadn't got them on him but gave up and handed me a squashed packet containing three whole cigarettes and one partly smoked. I took them, and though they weren't my usual brand, I looked forward to smoking them myself.

'Tell you what,' he said. 'I'll stop if you stop.'

'What?'

'I gave you mine. Now you give me yours.'

'And then what?'

I don't think I had ever seen him look so mischievous and triumphant. 'I'll destroy yours and you can destroy mine.'

'Throw them in the bin?' I'd done *that* before. *And* got them out again. And smoked them.

'Or,' he said, 'break em in little bits and put them down the toilet.'

I let him do it. I joined in and tore his squashed offering into fragments while he tidily broke my nearly full packet into neat quarters. He called Jojo away from the telly to join in the flushing ceremony.

'Do you swear by Almighty God,' he said, 'to not go out and buy more ciggies.'

'I don't believe in God,' I said.

He thought for a bit. 'Do you swear by my Granma then?'

'Do you?'

He even laughed at this point. 'I swear by my Almighty Granma,' he said, 'that I will not buy any more fags. Now you.'

'I swear,' I said – she was not *my* Granma and I did not know how to say it. 'Will that do?'

'No,' he said. 'Say, I swear by my sister Pauline –'

'All right.' We had gone too far for me to back out. 'I swear by my sister Pauline that I will not buy any more cigarettes.'

'Or smoke anyone else's.'

I sighed. 'Or smoke anyone else's.'

He signalled to Jojo to flush the toilet and there we were, non-smokers.

And these days I am grateful to him. Sometimes even now the feeling comes from nowhere, the dying for a fag feeling, but now I know it will go away if I let it. He achieved what Pauline never managed to do and as well saved me money over the last twelve years. Even a two-or-three-a-day habit adds up, and now, if I was living through lockdown and still a smoker I'd probably be up to fifty a day, just to pass the time.

Heidi changed too, that year after Pauline died. Before that she believed nothing could hurt her. She thought she could go through life doing what she wanted – men, children, responsibilities, none of these could touch her, or suffer from what she chose to do. I put it down to Pauline's way of parenting; it was too calm, too accommodating. Reasonable. She never let Heidi see how worried she was by the choices she made; she didn't lose her temper and have a good shout like I wanted to. 'Stay out of it Pam,' she used to say to me. 'You'll only make it worse if you get emotional.'

It was lucky that term was nearly over and my timetable was to some extent reduced. No more Year 11 teaching, no form tutor duties. Caroline was sympathetic and let me remove myself from the school trip (reward for good attendance) to Alton Towers, on the grounds that I was supporting my niece and her children in their hour of need. Jarvis and Jojo and I settled into a quiet routine. I left school early, not attending any meetings, and picked them up from their respective schools. When we got home Heidi would bring the two little ones and we would catch up on what had been happening – usually nothing except waiting in vain at the ruined house for someone to come and do a survey, give an estimate, make a pronouncement, suggest a date.

She would always bring a bag of washing and the children's clothes would be swishing away in the kitchen while we ate biscuits and Cassie bothered us to let her go outside, though it was cool and rainy and there was nothing for a child to do in my garden.

Heidi promised them a day out on Sunday, when Adam would be available with his big van. 'We'll go to Brid for the day,' she said. 'We'll let Pam have a bit of peace.'

'Pam likes us here,' said Jarvis. 'Don't you?'

'She can come with us,' said Cassie.

'It's all right,' I said. 'I need to catch up on some schoolwork.' Which was a small lie.

I was glad I hadn't gone with them as all day Sunday the rain fell steadily. I would have liked to do some gardening – it had been so wet that plants were leaning over as if exhausted and squadrons of slugs, black and brown and the disgusting greeny-yellow ones, had taken over the paths.

Monday morning it was still raining. When I woke up the light was grey, and rain was hitting the window like a percussion section. Every morning waking up was the same – there was a short space, maybe a second, maybe less – when everything seemed normal, right, as it should be, as it had always been, and then, like being smacked round the head with a bag of sand, it all came back. I realised the rain had been happening all night and that my sleep had been disturbed.

These days there's a similar thing. I wake up and wonder idly what I might do with the day, and then realise there is nothing I can do except stay at home, or walk round the block, speaking to no one, watch the news on TV, listen to it on the radio, which is never good. The numbers of dead people exceed what I can imagine; we are used to a disaster every so often, the reports of how many dead. Seventy-one for Grenfell Tower, ninety-six from the Hillsborough disaster, two hundred and forty, plus, for the Dale Dyke flood – these are what you might call numbers that can be grasped, cognitively. Two hundred and forty is roughly the number in one of our school Year Groups – 'Imagine,' I have said to them, 'imagine a Year assembly – that's how many people died in the Dale dyke flood.' Now, from the virus, it's more than two hundred and forty *every day* for weeks now, and the numbers keep being given out. Too many numbers to grasp – cases, tests, deaths – they slide past me like water, ungraspable.

I had told them at school that I would be late because I had to take Jojo to spend the day at the unit down in Hillsborough where he would be transferring to when he left his school. Whether he understood where he was going, whether he understood anything at all, no one ever really knew.

'And you're his mum?' said the manager.

'I'm his aunt,' I said. 'His great aunt actually.' I told her about Heidi being flooded out and temporarily homeless and having other children to get off to school, and also that I had to get off to work myself and didn't have time to look round the place. Then I set off back to school.

It was quite a quiet day. The kids weren't able to go out at break times, but they didn't even want to; the weather had subdued us all and made them sluggish and only good for leaning on walls in the corridors and in class, gazing out of windows, hypnotised by the relentless rain.

At the end of the day I avoided the staff meeting – one good thing – because I had to go and pick up Jojo, and I drove down towards Hillsborough. At Neepsend I was stopped because there was a barrier across the bridge and a lone policeman standing on it. Other cars were turning and making their way back up the hill. I parked up and went to tell him I needed to get through – vulnerable child waiting for me, et cetera.

'No chance madam,' he said. 'See that?' He pointed over the balustrade. 'The water's right up to the bridge. Stand where I am, you can feel it moving.'

I took a step forward, though he didn't expect or want me to, and he was right, the stone bridge, topped with two lanes of tarmac, was vibrating. Gently, but vibrating.

'Could go at any minute,' he said.

I turned to go. 'Hold on tight then,' I called back to him, and I laughed. It was a strange sensation.

I drove back up the hill so as to get into Hillsborough by a different road. The windscreen wipers were on at top speed, as if in a cloudburst, but this rain was steady and looked as if it could last for a week.

Things were no better at Leppings Lane; the road was already under water and barred to traffic. But pedestrians were walking through, in both directions. I parked the car again and walked towards the bridge, glad that my shoes were sensible but sorry that I had on my best grey trouser suit – having had it cleaned – and that it was going to get wet.

I was a trifle daunted when I got to the bridge. No one seemed to be thinking that it was about to be carried away and no one was being prevented from walking over it, but it was well under water and a person of my height would be in water almost up to their waist. A bunch of teenagers stood in the deepest part, looking over the side and shouting excitedly. One or two of them were known to me, from previous years, and among them I distinguished Daisy, but it was not the moment to think about her. The water was brown and flowing fast and I had to stand and gather some courage before I stepped into it.

If I stayed on the right hand side I figured I would be able to hold on to the railing.

A voice said to me, 'Do you think we should hold on to each other?'

'I think we'll be all right on our own,' I said, 'No need for us both to drown.'

Then I looked at her. She was exactly the sort of person I try to avoid. A retired lady, very small, full make-up, high-heeled shoes, expensive handbag. The sort of person who relies on other people.

'Please,' she said. 'I'm so nervous.'

So why do it, I said to myself. Just stay here, or go home. Then I thought, Pauline wouldn't say no. Then I thought, If Pauline was here *she* would be wearing high heels and carrying a handbag that cost a hundred pounds.

'Come on then,' I said.

She went next to the railings, holding on and inching along, and I took her left arm and tried not to be too obvious about hurrying her. I could feel the tug of the water pulling sideways on my legs.

'Oh, isn't it dreadful,' she was saying.

Shut up, I thought. Even Barbara wouldn't be moaning as much as you.

As we crossed over the deepest part I looked down into the river – it was the River Don here – and saw against the railings, heaps of debris – tree trunks, branches, twigs, litter – washed up against them.

'Oh look at that,' she cried out and took her hand off the railing to point at something. What it was she saw – a supermarket trolley? A message in a bottle? A kingfisher? – I was never to find out.

As she let go of the railing she slipped and went under. As she went under I was pulled down too. Someone – a man I think – tried to grab us but missed me. Maybe he got her, I never knew.

I was under water, I felt myself being carried by the water though I couldn't see where I was going; then my head was out again and I tried to take a breath and choked on what I'd already swallowed. It was seconds, that's all, it can't have been more than seconds, but it seemed endless, and then – this is what they told me later – I crashed into the balustrade on the other side and when people got hold of me I wasn't conscious.

I was all right. I came round before the men loaded me into the ambulance but one thing you can't ever do is sit up on a stretcher and say, Thanks all the same but I've got to go and pick up my nephew. Once you're in their clutches you have no autonomy whatever. Of course I was soaked through, vomiting water and had a bang on the back of my head that was tender and already making me think with longing of a paracetamol and my own bed. They took me to the hospital and I have to admit I felt pretty bad. My chest hurt and my leg hurt where something must have bashed into it. 'Just a bruise,' the doctor said, and listened again to my lungs.

I lay back on the bed and looked at the curtains of the cubicle and thought I might as well die, it wouldn't be a problem, and if I died today, tonight, tomorrow, I would never have to think again about what happened when Pauline died.

Of course I was nowhere near dying. A stout nurse came and took my details again.

'Date of birth,' said the nurse. I told her.

'Next Sunday,' she said. 'Not long. Doing anything nice?'

It occurred to me for the first time that I would be a year older – I would be fifty-seven – and Pauline would stay forever fifty-six. I would move further and further away from her with every year that passed.

I hoped to get away with not letting Heidi know, although it was a stupidly faint hope. I was sure the unit would have called her and told her that I hadn't arrived to pick up Jojo, and she would have had to deal with that emergency; I hoped she would think I'd been kept late at work, but of course, Jarvis would have to tell her that I wasn't at home. My car was parked at Wadsley Bridge, they would never find it.

They would try to ring my mobile but that would be downriver at Doncaster by now, and if I'd had it I doubt if it would have worked ever again. I was thinking slowly and confusedly but finally came to the conclusion that there was nothing I could do. Heidi was not in her own house; her mobile number was in my phone but not in my head, the landline in Pauline's house had been disconnected. And I was not allowed out of bed anyway.

They kept me there overnight, to keep an eye on me, they said. I lay there, doped, through the night and in the early hours I dreamed about Pauline. Nothing happened in my dream, only that she was there, and behind her, everyone else, Dad, Auntie Vi, Vincent (my brother, not the dog) and then an unknown woman stepped forward and stood beside Pauline and I knew it was our mother, and then the nurses began rattling about, changing their shift, and the dream went back to where it came from in my disordered brain.

This is another thing about hospitals – they operate on a different clock to everyone else. 'You'll be discharged,' they say, and you start to get out of bed, a bit bruised and stiff but ready to free up the bed for some other poor soul, and they say, 'after the doctor has seen you.' And you wait and eventually the doctor – not the one you saw before – comes and says you're good to go and they say, 'But you need someone to come and get you. We can't let you go on your own.'

'I'll call a taxi,' I said, but that wasn't good enough.

'Relatives?'

I went back over my reasoning of the previous night and came to the same conclusion.

These days of course it is rank sacrilege to say a word against anyone remotely connected to the NHS. Even the stroppy, gossiping receptionist at our local practice is now a fully canonised being. And don't get me wrong; I'm happy for it to be that way if it stops the wholesale selling off of our service. And if it secured them better funding so much the better. Come to think of it schools could do with some as well.

'I'll see what the ward manager wants us to do,' she said and disappeared. I thought about sneaking out and I would have done if my clothes had been available to me. After a wait another person came to see me. I had to go through my name and address and date of birth all over again, as if I was an imposter trying to sleep in someone else's bed, and then she said, 'There's been someone enquiring for you. Someone called Heidi Dearly?'

'She's my niece,' I said firmly. 'She's the nearest relation I've got in Sheffield.'

'I'll call her back,' said the woman.

She didn't return to tell me the outcome of the phone call and I couldn't be sure that she'd even made it, but after what seemed a long wait, during which other people got lunch but I didn't because I had officially left, Heidi appeared, along with Jojo and the baby, and took me home.

'If you go down by Wadsley Bridge,' I said, 'I can pick up my car.' The keys, miraculously, were still in my possession.

'No way,' she said. 'You're not fit to drive.'

'Oh come on,' I said.

'No,' she said. 'Adam will go down later and get it for you. You've been concussed, you've got to rest.'

I wondered how long Adam would last – though a much more pleasant human being than the likes of Gavin, he seemed to spend every waking hour running errands and doing quite major jobs for Heidi and her children. I thought he might get tired of it.

It was however a good feeling to be home. The phone was blinking away and I would have listened to the messages but Heidi was in full, Pauline-like, knowing best sort of mode and made me go and lie on the sofa. I heard them though as she played them back – all from school, asking where I was, becoming more anxious as they went along. I heard her ring the school and tell them what had happened and that I would be off for the rest of the week. She brought in cups of tea and a cheese sandwich. Jojo turned on the TV, the baby practised his walking from one piece of furniture to another.

'What a week,' she said. 'What a year. One thing after another. Honestly Pam I really thought the worst had happened. And we'd got the insurance assessor coming and he couldn't get through so I was waiting for him to come, and the woman where Jojo was – she was ringing me up saying – first of all, where were we, and then, don't try to get there, and then, she was going to take him home with her. Poor lamb, he was properly confused.'

'So did she? Take him home?'

'Yes, but Adam went and got him. Had to go right round as far as Barnsley to find a way across.'

'I'm sorry,' I said. 'I couldn't help it.' I was feeling sorry for myself now, rather than grateful to be all right.

'You couldn't help it,' she agreed. 'I wasn't blaming you. Jojo's feeling OK today, you're back home, we're no further forward with our insurance claim but everything's OK.' She finished off her tea. 'The thing is,' she said, 'I'm never going to feel secure again. One thing after another, ever since Mum died. It's like walking through quicksand.'

'I know,' I said. And then I must have gone to sleep.

For the rest of the week I did hardly anything. I could not have believed that a bang on the head could cause such lethargy, such strange episodes of helpless weeping. Not even weeping really, just water flowing out of my eyes – turning on the waterworks, as Vi used to say if We ever tried it. The worst thing that set me off was the local news, with all the pictures of the ruined homes. I have to say it didn't do Heidi any good either. Two people in Sheffield actually died, one a boy of Jarvis' age who fell into a river, and one an elderly man who was swept away downtown. And further downstream a poor young man got his foot somehow caught in a drain and had to watch the waters rising and engulfing him until he drowned. That really was the most awful. Jarvis and I shouted at the television – 'Get an axe. Chop his foot off.' Someone tell me why that feels worse than five hundred people dying in one day, in England, of a virus.

Heidi spent most of the days with me, only going to the bungalow when the little ones needed to be put to bed, and by then Jarvis and Jojo were with me, getting through lorry-loads of biscuits and watching strange programmes on TV that I had never seen before. Cassie was fascinated by the story of my adventure and rescue. 'Why didn't you swim?' she asked. The truth was that I couldn't. Pauline and I had never learned to swim. When We were at school they tried to make us but We always found an excuse and if they insisted then one or the other of us would have a nose bleed. We were prone to these anyway and knew how to make them happen. (Hold your nostrils tight shut and blow – not that I want anyone to try it.) Then the other one would have to take the one dripping with blood to the toilets to get cleaned up and We could easily make it last the length of the swimming lesson.

Frank Midgely called, and Caroline, bringing flowers and chocolates and messages of sympathy and support from my colleagues. I had never expected such a thing, happening so soon after my previous misfortune and absence; I thought they would write me off as nothing but a nuisance, looking for special treatment.

'You misjudge them,' said Caroline when I told her how I felt. 'Nobody thinks you're skiving. People know what an effort you've been making all this year. People admire you for getting on with the job.'

It was hard to believe her – in fact I didn't – but it was nice of her to say it.

Trev popped in as well, on Friday afternoon while Heidi was out collecting the children.

'I heard about it,' he said. 'Just wanted to make sure you're all right.'

'I'm fine,' I said, and to prove it I made him a cup of tea, and we sat in the kitchen and looked out at the garden which was still sodden but on that day basking in sunshine.

'Need any help with the garden?' he said. I thought I could detect a yearning for getting his fingers in the soil.

'I don't *need* it,' I said, 'but if you wanted to you could come and give me a hand with it next week after school. Assuming the rains stops for long enough.'

Heidi came with Jojo and the little ones, and made more tea, and we had to explain about our temporary living arrangements. Then, dragging his school bag along the ground, Jarvis appeared.

'Wow, Trev,' he said. 'What are you doing here?'

'Just visiting,' said Trev. 'Came to see how your Auntie's doing after her little escapade. How are you, Jarv?'

'All right,' said Jarvis and disappeared to watch TV with Jojo.

When he came back, on a mission for biscuits, Trev was standing up ready to go. 'I didn't know you knew my Auntie,' said Jarvis. 'It's her birthday on Sunday.'

'I thought it was tomorrow,' said Trev.

'Oh no,' said Heidi. 'My mum and my auntie are too special for that.'

'I thought they were twins,' he said.

'Tell him Pam,' said Heidi and I had to explain again about the inconvenient midnight that had divided her birth from mine.

'That must be pretty rare,' he said.

'I guess so,' I said. 'We always believed We were pretty special. When We were little I mean.'

'Tell about your middle names,' said Jarvis, so I had to do that bit as well, and I did it without crying and Trev made suitable remarks and Heidi invited him round for cake on Sunday.

Adam turned up then with the bad news that the brook at the end of Heidi's garden had overflowed again, flooding into the already flooded cellar.

Two girls, Daisy and Nessa, from my form – my old form – came to see me, bringing more chocolate.

'I saw it,' Daisy told me. 'The boys I was with – you know, Gaz and Liam – they pulled you out. I did too. We thought you were dead.'

No such luck, I thought. But I thanked her anyway and told her she could bring the boys to see me so that I could thank them. If they wanted to come. I did not expect that they would and I was right.

The girls told me what I already knew, that the children from our school had by and large escaped the worst of the flood. Up on the hill where we were it was possible not to believe how much water there had been in the valleys. But Daisy, who lived near Hillsborough Park, described how the water stopped only inches away from flooding their cellar. 'And you know Ricky, lives near the Wednesday ground? All those houses – completely ruined. Winn Gardens too.'

All over the city families living near the swollen rivers were in the same predicament as Heidi was, and not one of *them*, I was willing to bet, had a spare house to move in to. I said as much to her when the girls had gone and she was giving the kids their tea.

'I know I'm lucky,' she said. 'I know I've got nothing to complain about, compared to other people. But it doesn't stop me being totally hacked off. And I'm getting worried about Jojo. There's something not right.'

'One day at a time,' I said. So many people had said that to me that I knew it was the thing to say. I can't say it had ever helped me though, and it didn't seem to help Heidi.

Floods have become a fact of life now, in the north, in the west, everywhere. Only before last Christmas a whole village had to be evacuated not far away from here because a dam was threatening to burst. A happier ending this time though, because there are experts who monitor these things, and instruments that tell the experts how dangerous the situation is and helicopters to drop great bags of sand onto the compromised section, and phones to tell people what to do and an internet to let the whole world know. They did not have to send a boy on a horse down to Sheffield to bring back the engineer, who in turn did not even have an electric torch to help him judge how serious the breach was.

Terry never did get back to me and I never tried to get in touch with him, which I could have done, through mutual acquaintances. It didn't bother me, it wasn't important. Someone told me he'd gone to live in France.

So our birthdays arrived, though for the first time in my life it was mine only. My brothers and sisters sent me cards, and Alan and Maureen treated me to a phone call – I did not let on that I had had an accident; couldn't bear the prospect of all that sympathy and offers to come and stay, and all the 'what a blessing that –' and the 'we'll be thinking of you,' and the 'are you sure you don't need looking after?'

Anyway, we had – I had – a muted kind of birthday. In the past Pauline had been in the habit of baking a large cake and having Heidi and all the children, and me, round for a sort of party tea on the 30th which was properly her birthday, not mine. Then I would have gone home and she would have gone out for a meal with one, or some, of her friends. I was often invited, but I never went. My own birthday, the next day, usually went without any fuss, though some years Pauline would bring the remains of the cake round and We would have a glass of something with it. This year, in the circumstances, Heidi did her best. There was a cake – not a home-made one it's true, but one from Morrison's, and Cassie sang Happy Birthday to me. Trev came – just popped in, he said, and helped to eat the cake. I was off the sofa by now; I was going back to school for the remaining two and a bit weeks of term.

'I'm worried about Jojo,' said Heidi. 'You know what he's like about changes to his routine. He's not settled.' She was just getting ready to take the little ones down to the bungalow.

'You wouldn't expect him to be,' I said. 'He's OK when he's here.'

'He's OK when he's got me or Jarvis with him,' she said. 'But I can tell there's something wrong. He's fidgety.'

'He's had a lot happen to him,' I said. 'It will take time.'

'He's supposed to be starting at the Centre soon,' she said. 'He didn't have the best experience there did he, not being able to get home at the end of the day.'

'He may not remember,' I said, though I knew as I said it that Jojo was famous in the family for his memory for people and places and the tiniest of incidents, especially ones that scared or upset him. Heidi did not bother to argue with me.

School, once I was back there, was fine, though tiring. Work Experience was over. Exams were over. Various sports days and extra-curricular outings had come and gone. It truly was the last leg of the year and there was that familiar feeling of 'Where did it all go?' I was fifty seven; I had just completed my thirty-sixth year of teaching.

Getting to know Pauline's form group was a diversion. I knew most of them of course, from having taught them History at some previous point in their school careers, and from discussions with Pauline over the last four years. They seemed to have less character about them than my old class, dull and docile I found them, but at least there seemed to be no Kane-and-Josh-type characters to worry about.

They came into my classroom looking around them as if they'd never seen it before. For four years their form room – their home room as they say in the States – had been the big kitchen room that Pauline taught in with its cookers and sinks along the walls and the drawers and cupboards full of pots and pans and dishcloths and tea towels, and the posters on the walls reminding them to wash their hands and how to dispose separately of the different sorts of rubbish. And there would have been Pauline, in her overall and hairnet which she always wore at work, sitting calmly behind her desk and marking them in on the electronic register, fully confident that they would behave sensibly. She was good, Pauline, good at her job. No fuss, no histrionics from her and no showing off from the kids.

Obviously my room was going to be different from that. Ordinary desks and blue plastic chairs, bookshelves of textbooks, piles of exercise books on my desk. My posters on the walls changed often, according to what various year groups were supposed to be studying. I had taken some down already for the end of term, but Hitler was still balefully looking down, and slaves in chains were still up high where I couldn't reach without the caretaker's stepladder.

As the week went on, instead of becoming calm, Jojo was getting more and more unhappy and disturbed. Maybe, or maybe not, it was because he understood that he was leaving his special school where he had been since he was five, and was transferring to an adult unit, possibly for the rest of his life. Maybe it was living in my house instead of his own that was upsetting him. Maybe he was anxious because Heidi wasn't sleeping in the same house as him. He couldn't tell us in words, and we couldn't know whether the reassuring words we said to him made a difference. It seemed that they didn't. He was restless as soon as Heidi went down to the bungalow to put the children to bed. If Jarvis left his side he muttered angrily and threw the remote across the room. He resisted going to bed, and in the night I could hear him waking and moaning, and then Jarvis' sleepy voice telling him it was all right. Jarvis was a hero, and I was grateful to him that I didn't have to get out of bed and deal with anything. It took a while to get back to sleep though, for all three of us. Then, one evening as Heidi was preparing to go back to the bungalow, Jojo stationed himself at the front door and would not let her past. He was as tall as her now and for all he didn't weigh as much he was surprisingly strong. She was holding the baby and a bag of clean washing; Cassie was beside her.

'Jo,' called Jarvis from the front room. 'Come and see this.'

But he was not to be diverted. He made a grab for the baby, reasoning I suppose that his mother would not leave without him. She fended him off and said to Cassie in a low voice, 'We'll go out the back door. Stay next to me.'

But Jojo made a grab for Cassie then and made her scream. Heidi got them out of the back door but I couldn't stop Jojo following. They were now standing in the street having an argument, Heidi speaking slowly and firmly, Jojo, understanding or not, shaking his head gravely and deliberately, as if he could convince her that way.

'Why don't you let him go with you?' said Jarvis, from the doorstep. 'I'll come and get him later, when it's bedtime.'

It seemed a reasonable plan, but later, when Jarvis and I went to fetch him we found that he was still in an agitated state.

'He's looking for Mum,' said Heidi. 'He's just going from room to room, like he's searching for something, and it must be her. And he's hitting himself – he hasn't done that for years. I don't know what to do with him.'

We got him home eventually, by a mixture of bribes and threats and pulling firmly at his clothes, but though he went to bed quite calmly he was awake again and wailing in the night, and the next evening we had a repeat performance.

'What can we do?' said Heidi. 'I can't stay here all night, I can't leave the children to be with him. We can't go home – it feels like we'll never get to go home.'

(The insurance assessor, when he had finally come, had not been hopeful. There were now more than a thousand flooded homes, and almost as many flooded businesses – well, we knew that from the TV news – which meant that not only were the assessors rushed off their feet but every builder, floorer, plasterer, plumber, electrician and kitchen fitter in the county would have work that would take them months to get on top of.

'Look,' said Heidi, 'I can do it myself. Or my boyfriend can do it. All I need is the money.'

But for money it seems you need estimates and every tradesman was dealing with a backlog. And then you need invoices and receipts and guarantees. Adam, when I saw him, did not give an opinion on how long it would take – he was actually a surveyor, though of roads and bridges rather than houses, and he was busy himself going round the city identifying problems. I still worried that though he was too polite to complain, the whole stressful situation would drive him away from Heidi.)

She sat back down in a chair and seemed to have given up. Jojo stayed by the door, one eye on the TV and one on his mother. The baby was flushed and cranky. Jarvis and I stood helplessly; I felt as if I was in the way, as if I was the cause of this stand-off, by not being good enough, by not being Pauline, by not, actually, loving any of them enough to make any difference.

'Can you speak to the school?' I said. 'Can the psychiatrist help?'

'I did that,' she said. 'The woman just said he needed stability. I could have told *her* that. But how can I give it him? We haven't had stability all year. And he's upsetting Cassie too. I don't want her to be scared of him.'

'If I had another bed,' I said. 'You could stay here tonight. But there isn't really enough room.' I remembered my night sleeping with Cassie and didn't want to repeat it.

'If it was only one night we could manage,' Heidi said. 'But one night isn't going to solve it. What would we do tomorrow, and the next day. And week. And month.' She began to cry. She was always like me in that way, easy unstoppable tears.

'I tell you what,' said Jarvis. 'You stay here, Mum, with Jo, and I'll sleep in Granma's with the littlies. Or just with Cassie. We can bring the cot up here.'

It was not an idea that appealed to me. I was getting on with Heidi OK but I didn't want her around for even more of the time. I said, 'That's not really fair on you Jarv. You're not really old enough to be left in charge of Cassie.'

'Well I've done it plenty of times,' he said.

I thought of how none of this was my fault. I thought about what Pauline might have done; she would have come to stay with me – and I would not have minded her staying with me at all – and let Heidi and her whole family have her bungalow for as long as they needed to. And Jojo would have been able to see his Granma often enough not to have to search for her. If only.

Jarvis was still thinking. 'This might work. You come and live here with us. And Auntie Pam – cos there won't be room for her here – she can go and stay in the bungalow.'

I was outraged. Auntie Pam was outraged. No one cared about me. This was *my* house. All my stuff was here – and a lot of Pauline's too. I had had an accident. An accident brought about by having to fetch Jojo. Why couldn't they *make* Jojo understand that Granma was gone and there was no point searching for her and getting upset. Or if upset, no point in kicking off. He wasn't my responsibility, he was Heidi's. This was *my* house. She was lucky, bloody lucky, to have a place to stay. Jojo was *her* responsibility, not mine. It was her problem.

I didn't say anything. There was a long pause while I didn't say anything, and then Heidi said, as if Jarvis hadn't said what he said, 'I expect he'll settle down. Another night or two and he'll get used to it.' She would take him back to the bungalow tonight.

So she did and Jarvis went too. I had my house to myself for the first time in weeks.

I reviewed in my mind what I possessed. I had two bedrooms that *were* bedrooms, my room which had a single bed – as I had never had any need for a double – and the guest room where the two boys had been sleeping in twin beds. My smallest upstairs room, that people used to call a boxroom, was nominally a study, though at the moment was still like the back room of a charity shop, heaped with disparate articles of varying degrees of usefulness. Downstairs I had a kitchen, a small and rarely used dining room and the front room where the TV was. Though I had put away some of my stuff – even thrown away a few things, there was still a lot of stuff lying around taking up space. In the front room there was a three-piece suite, of which the settee was not comfortable enough for an adult to spend the night and anyway not long enough to accommodate either of the boys. I thought of the people across the city who were being forced to live with relatives, probably in even more difficult circumstances.

But I also had what I always referred to as 'the other bit.' I had to stop myself from thinking about it as a constant reproach. It had been built on the side of my house as some sort of granny flat and it was the reason I bought the house in the first place, in the belief that pretty soon Heidi would leave home and Pauline would be pleased to come and share my house with me again. The fact that Heidi did leave home before Jojo was born but that Pauline then – without consultation with me – sold her flat and bought her bungalow – that fact hurt me more than I was prepared to let her know. I never used those two extra rooms; I never considered them as part of my home. They were full of junk – old furniture, piles of books and papers, unwanted duty gifts from people in the family, some not even opened, but mostly stuff that belonged to school – tents and mattresses from the days when we used to do camping trips, props and scenery from the days when we had the energy to put on school productions, ancient slide projectors and boxes of videos that someone was going to put on DVD but had never got round to. It was not a space that anyone would consider sleeping in, any more than you might consider a garden shed an appropriate bedroom. It would take weeks to empty it and when empty it would not be inviting; it had never had carpet or curtains and had never been cleaned or tidied in Jojo's lifetime.

When I went pick up the children next morning Heidi opened the door looking bedraggled and dull, and said nothing when I asked her how he had been. I didn't ask again in front of Cassie but after we dropped her at nursery I asked Jarvis how it had been. He too, now I looked at him, was looking tired.

'Not good,' he said. He glanced behind to see if Jojo was listening. 'Throwing things,' he said quietly. 'Bit noisy.'

It was the last day at school for all of us; six weeks of summer holiday in front of us. I didn't stay at school for the end of term festivities – kids going home at lunchtime, presentations to staff who were leaving and retiring, everyone leaving school early and going to the pub. I couldn't face all those endings so I said goodbye to Frank Midgeley and went home as soon as the kids were off the premises. Soon after, Heidi arrived with her children and her bag of washing. We drank tea and nothing was said about the night they had had. I was waiting to see if she would say anything about the night that would soon be upon us but she didn't say much at all. I hoped she had managed to get some sleep during the day, but I didn't ask her.

Once again Jojo made a big fuss and in the end they all went back to the bungalow and I had a second night on my own. After they had gone and before I went to bed – I really wasn't sleepy at all – I had a go at organising the piles of stuff from the small bedroom. It was in my mind that maybe we could do some shuffling around, bring the mattresses up and somehow all fit in. I pulled down the loft ladder and – even though I was on my own in the house – transferred most of the stuff up there, some of it in boxes, some in bags, some just chucked through the hatch to be dealt with at some later date. It was after one when I finished and the little room looked empty and surprised at itself. But it still had my desk and lap-top and two chairs, and a bookshelf of text books (some very out of date) and two big bags of school work that I intended to get on top of in the next six weeks. Even a single mattress on the floor would only just fit in.

On Saturday Adam took the family out for the day. I did some washing and hung it outside. I ate meals on my own for the first time in three weeks. The house was quiet, like the weather, grey and overcast, but dry. I wandered round the garden and wondered if Trev might show up but he didn't.

When the phone rang it was Barbara – obviously her turn to waste a Saturday afternoon on me.

'How's Heidi doing?'

'She's fine,' I said.

'And the kids? Must be unsettling for them.'

'They're OK,' I said.

'Maureen and me,' she said, 'we were wondering whether – now it's the holidays – whether they'd like to come down and visit. You know, all of them. Have a break from everything.'

'I don't know,' I said. 'You'd have to ask her.'

'Well I will,' she said. 'I just thought I'd run it past you first. You know the situation better than we do. They could stay at Jim's – there's loads of room. Verona would love to have them.'

She rang off soon after that. I was indignant that she hadn't asked how I was, but then I remembered that I hadn't let them know about the accident. I had deliberately kept it from them and it was too late now to get any sympathy.

On Sunday Heidi rang to ask if she could bring her washing to put in my machine. She looked more tired than ever.

'He's taken a door off its hinges,' she said. 'He's getting destructive. I daren't let him out of my sight. He's breaking stuff, Jarv's stuff, Cassie's toys. It's like he took it really quietly when Mum died and now all this has just tipped him over.'

'Could he have something to calm him down?' I said. It crossed my mind that he could be admitted into a mental hospital and sedated but I knew better than to say it, and to tell the truth I didn't like the idea anyway. 'Valium or something?'

'I don't know,' she said.

'Where is he now?'

'He's gone for a walk with Jarv. They'll be down at the park. He likes that. No memories I suppose.'

'And he's going to the Centre tomorrow?'

'I'll try,' she said. 'I don't want him to lose his place. Maybe you could take Cassie to nursery and keep an eye on Baby while Jarv and I try and get him there?'

I had no grounds for saying no.

I dropped Cassie off – she seemed quite unaffected by all the changes that were going on – and drove back home with the baby. On an impulse I put him in the pushchair and walked though the streets to the park. It was too early in the day for it to be full of teenagers and we had it more or less to ourselves. I put him in one of the baby swings and pushed him for what seemed like an hour, but when I looked at my watch only five minutes had gone by. How do people do it, I wondered, when childcare is so unimaginably boring. He didn't want to come out of the swing so I pushed for another five minutes, and then tried again. This time, sensing that I was not in charge of the situation, he put up more resistance. He stiffened himself into an unbending straight line so that I couldn't lift him through the bars; he protested as well, a sort of outraged roar, and went very red in the face. I recalled that Heidi had behaved in much the same way when thwarted by me – though her mother was much better at talking her round. Bribery may have been used as well.

'Look,' I said, and pointed. 'Shall we go on the roundabout?' I did wonder whether I was letting myself in for a whole morning of playground activity but if I could just get him out of the swing he would be at my mercy since I was that much bigger than him, and probably more cunning too. I hoped so anyway. He fell for the roundabout, and I used the same trick to get him off it and on to a rocking horse and then a climbing frame. That was not such a good idea since he was too little to be able to climb, gave up and set off in a tottering run to make a bid for getting back in the swing, which was clearly his first love.

When I finally got him home Heidi and Jarvis were waiting.

'You'll have to get a new phone,' said Heidi. 'We didn't know where you were.'

'Well, I'm here now. How did it go?'

'He's there. Not happy, but he's there. They seem to know what they're doing. Going to have a short day today so can I leave little Jay with you while I go and fetch him after lunch.'

Once again, there was no possibility of saying no.

However, in the afternoon I walked him round in the pushchair until he fell asleep and the I parked him in the garden and pottered about nearby, pulling up weeds and deadheading roses. I was not surprised to see Trev coming through the side gate; I put my finger to my lips to tell him not to make a noise.

'How's it going?' he said.

I told him.

'So Heidi's house –?'

'Completely uninhabitable. No change from the last time we told you.'

'Lucky she's got her mother's place then.'

'Of course she's lucky, she knows she is, but it doesn't feel lucky when your children are in two different places and you've got no furniture, and now –' I told him about Jojo.

'I wish I could help,' he said.

'Why should you?' I said. 'She's better off than most, as you said. You've no reason to help her more than some other family.' I didn't say it but I thought it – What do you think *I'm* doing?

'Well,' he said. 'I wish I could do something for Pauline's sake. She's not had an easy life, Heidi hasn't.'

Well, *I* thought she had.

Trev went soon after that and Heidi came back with the others and we fell into our usual routine, washing machine on, mugs of tea, biscuits, worried conversations.

'You know Pam,' she said, 'it's not only Jojo who's struggling with all of this.'

'Cassie seems fine,' I said. 'I'm very impressed with her; takes it all in her stride. And he –' I indicated Jayden who was sitting in the floor chewing a wooden spoon – 'he's too young to know what's happening.'

'It's me though,' she said, 'being in Mum's house – it's surreal. She's everywhere. I see her. Or, I don't quite see her but I nearly see her, do you know what I mean? It's like she's there but I've just missed seeing her. Do you know what I mean?'

'No,' I said.

'Like a presence,' she said. 'In her house it's sort of like she's still there, but I can't catch her being there.'

'There are no ghosts,' I said.

'Not a ghost. Nothing you can see. A presence, that's all.'

She'd used that word – presence – twice now and I was envious, because all I had was an absence.

'I can't sleep properly,' she said. 'Suddenly, I'm wide awake, as if I've heard something, or as if I've just missed seeing something, or as if someone's just opened a door, or shut one.'

All this was pretty ridiculous, I thought, but if Jojo was experiencing the same sort of thing then it was understandable that he might be bothered by it. I did not know what I could say or do. I looked at her hard to try and make sure that she wasn't just saying all this to put pressure on me to swap houses, and she looked so defeated and worn out that I felt properly sorry for her. Her skin was rough and her eyes were red round the edges and her hair – which is usually glossy and smooth – was rough as well, dry and unwashed.

Even so, there was going to be no exchange of houses.

'I'm going to have to tell those people they can't have the bungalow,' she said, in a more upbeat tone, as if it was a change of subject.

I too had had this thought. There was no point selling off a perfectly liveable property and ending up homeless.

Later that evening she phoned. 'Pam. Could you come round?' There was crashing in the background.

When I got there Jarvis was sitting on Jojo's chest. An assortment of odd chairs were lying on their backs, mugs were lying in tea puddles on the floor. The TV was on but with no sound. Everyone was very quiet. Jojo was lying still and silent; Jarvis was managing to look quite nonchalant about the fact that he had his brother's hands pinned to the carpet. Heidi and I stood in the doorway of the sitting room, watching while nothing happened. Cautiously Jarvis shifted his weight as if he was going to get up. Jojo made a grunting noise and tried to throw him off; Jarvis resumed his former position.

'What I think we should do, 'Heidi said to me, in a low voice as if Jojo could understand her if he heard, 'is, you and me get hold of his arms so Jarv can have a rest.'

I righted the chairs in the room, which seemed to make Jojo restless and worried me that he might want to knock them over again. Heidi turned on the TV sound and Jojo twisted his head to see the screen, where some sort of vehicle was careering around a race track. Jarvis got off him slowly as Heidi and I took an arm each and led him to a chair.

'He'll be all right now,' said Jarvis, settling on the chair next to him.

'Until the next time,' said Heidi.

I told Trev about the episode when he popped in next day.

'So,' he said, 'what are you going to do?'

'There's nothing I can do,' I said. 'I'm not a psychiatrist.'

'If,' he said, and stopped.

'If what,' I said.

'Nothing,' he said. 'I know it's none of my business.'

I knew what he had been going to say. If Pauline were in my situation, she would do it. She would give up her house. She would put herself out, she wouldn't mind how much it cost her, in money and time and upheaval.

I knew what I would have said to him in reply. Heidi was not my responsibility, she was a grown up woman, she was responsible for herself and for her children. That was point number one. Two, it was bad enough having them all wandering in and out of my house whenever they felt like it; I did not like my own living space taken up with great big boys and tiny children and all their paraphernalia and their noisy demands. Three, a house swap could go on for months, with no firm date for ending; everything was uncertain. Four, suppose Jojo carried on being 'unsettled' in my house and started wrecking it. Five, how would we move all my stuff? Six, I had lived in that house for more years than I hadn't lived in it; it was my home, the garden was my garden, the view out of the windows was my view; I was totally committed to staying there until they carried me out feet first. Seven, it was MY HOUSE. I couldn't say that often enough to myself. MY HOUSE. MINE.

I looked around the kitchen where we were sitting. Every single item, every spoon and mug and saucepan, every chip on every piece of crockery, every scratch on the work surface, every splash on the tiles was telling me the same thing. This was my house. I did not want to leave it even for a week. 'It's all I have left.' The words came into my head and wanted to be spoken but I stopped myself because I did not want Trev to think I was being dramatic.

Instead I said, 'You were going to tell me Pauline would do it.'

He seemed to consider before he replied. 'She would, wouldn't she. She wouldn't have to think twice about it. It doesn't have to be for ever.'

'Look,' I said. 'Heidi has a two bedroom bungalow to live in. She's bloody lucky, in the circumstances. She probably wouldn't want to swap anyway. Jojo will get over it in a day or two.'

'If –' he said again.

'If what?'

'Suppose he doesn't.'

'He will.'

Trev twitched the corners of his mouth in what I suppose was an attempt at a smile. 'Let's hope so,' he said.

To be fair to Heidi – on this occasion she deserved fairness – she had not said anything further. She had appeared, even, to stay out of my way, and not in a manner that made me think she was in a huff about it. Jarvis, too, said nothing more about changing houses except to reassure me that he was not being haunted by the ghost of Pauline.

'I expect I got used to it,' he said, 'when I was there with that Alice.'

'Do you ever see her?' I said. 'Alice, I mean?' I occasionally wondered about her and her suicidal plans.

'They say she's coming back to school in September,' he said. 'But she's not in any of my classes. I hope.'

And then there was another development.

Heidi and the kids had eaten at my house, and Adam appeared as we were clearing the plates away, looking anxious and slightly furtive, making signs to Heidi to go outside with him. She took the baby with her and the other three sat down in a row on my settee and waited for Jojo to decide what to watch. Nobody, these days, knowingly upset Jojo; we tiptoed round him, watchfully.

Heidi eventually came back in, without Adam, also looking a bit agitated, a bit elated, a bit anxious.

'It's all right,' she said. 'Not a big thing.' As if I might have been worrying. 'It's just Adam needs somewhere to sleep tonight. Well, not just tonight.'

'Flooded out?' I said sarcastically, but she ignored me.

It turned out that Adam's wife had reached whatever point it is in a relationship where a person feels they've had enough. Who she was and how things had been for her and Adam, and whether or not she had known that he had taken up with Heidi, and whether or not he had had previous extra-maritals – all of these things I did not know, and was never to know. All I knew was what they told me – that he needed somewhere to sleep that night, and somewhere to live thereafter.

Jarvis looked quite pleased about it; Jojo and the little ones of course did not grasp the situation. I was wondering how they would all fit in down at the bungalow.

'Look,' I said. 'Why don't we give it another go, Jojo and Jarvis sleeping here? He might have got over it by now. Whatever it was.'

Heidi and Jarvis looked doubtful, then hopeful.

'Worth a try?' said Adam.

We tried to be as calm and casual as it was possible to be during the rest of the evening. Heidi took the little ones down to the bungalow and put them to bed. Then Adam went down there to stay with them while she came back to spend a little time with Jojo. He had been untroubled, I thought, while she was gone.

We all sat for a while watching a programme about police cars chasing young men in cars and arresting them for being drug dealers. I thought of Jarvis and Alice behind Tesco's bins, hiding from similar people. Then Heidi stood up and said that she was going now and it would soon be time for the boys to go to bed. 'Auntie Pam will make you some hot chocolate,' she said. 'Be good now.'

She gave Jojo a small kiss on the cheek and touched Jarvis gently on his head, and then, quietly and slowly, let herself out of the house.

All was calm. They drank their hot chocolate. They watched another programme – someone on a long foreign train. I didn't pay any attention; I was looking through the list of who would be in my next year's GCSE group and wondering how I could make the causes of the First World War interesting – to *me* even if not to the kids.

The boys, after some chivvying, went to bed. So did I, and I was just at that point where I was neither quite asleep nor anything like awake when it all started to kick off in their room. Jarvis was shouting at Jojo to stop it, stop it. When I stumbled into their room he, Jarv, was trying to burrow under the duvet to avoid the pummelling he was getting. Somehow, the silence with which Jojo was going at him made it more problematical. I got between them, which is what you can usually do safely with a pair of fighting boys if you're a woman, and although Jojo didn't stop trying to hit his brother, Jarvis was able to wriggle out of bed and get to the door. There he stopped, not wanting to leave me alone with the situation. He stood at the door and his thin white legs sticking out of his boxer shorts should have made me laugh but in fact almost made me cry. I can't explain.

'What's up?' I said.

'Dunno,' he said. 'He just started on me. He's never done that before.'

Jojo was standing where he had been, looking down at his brother's bed as if he thought he should still be there.

'Go and sleep in my bed,' I said. 'I'll stay here with him.'

'He won't do that,' said Jarvis. 'He needs me with him.'

'Then he'll have to learn,' I said. It was harsh but true. 'You won't always be living in the same house as him. You won't always be sharing a bedroom.'

'Why not?' said Jarvis.

'Because you will grow up and have a life,' I said.

212

I guided Jojo back into bed and covered him up as if he was a baby.

'I'll sit here,' I said, whether he understood me or not. 'I'll sit here on Jarv's bed until you go to sleep.' I turned the light out. 'Everything's all right,' I added, just to pretend it was.

We all got some sleep in the end. Jojo was restless and I was aware, even when nearly asleep myself, of him turning and shifting, and muttering in a way that made me tense in case he got up and started all over again. When I heard my alarm go off in the other room I had to drag myself out of a sleep that had not been nearly long enough or sound enough. When I saw Jarvis at breakfast he looked pretty ragged too.

'I'm OK,' he said softly but he did not look at me at all and I knew what he was thinking. A word from me and this drama could be at an end. If it had to go on, indefinitely, it would be my fault. What they wanted was a house big enough for all of them and one where Jojo would be able to calm down, and where they could all go back to normal and be a family again. What I wanted did not weigh a great deal against their need. I could have said that I wanted what *I* wanted – my house, my own house which was *mine,* and mine alone – more fiercely than they wanted what they wanted, but there were six of them and only one of me. Six of them plus the wishes – the truth of which I fully accepted – of Pauline. Pauline would have camped out in the garden for the rest of her life if she thought her family would benefit from it, and here I was, struggling to agree to an arrangement which would still provide me with a roof and a civilised home. And they were my family too, less closely than they were Pauline's but close enough. Genetically speaking Heidi was as much mine as Pauline's.

Heidi and Adam have never gone back to live in Chapeltown – why would they? That little house was repaired and made good and then rented out; these days Jarvis and Paige live there. Heidi, she tells me, puts the rent that they pay into a separate account so that she can give it back to them one day when they need it.

My house, the one I can see through the bare branches of the lime trees in winter, is a very different place from what it was when it was mine. From the front, quite recognisable, although the front garden has been paved to allow for two cars to be parked there. Inside it is tidy, downstairs at least, and modern and stylish. There is an extra bedroom up in the roof where Cassie sleeps and entertains her friends and does whatever teenagers these days do with their phones and their tablets. Jayden has my old bedroom though in normal times he's barely at home, having more important things to do, like playing football and hanging out with his friends. The kitchen has been extended and knocked through into the dining room; there is a downstairs shower room, and the shed-like 'extra bit' has been made into a sort of bedsit for Jojo so that he can feel a bit more grownup. He used to share it with Jarvis before Paige was on the scene, but now seems content to spend his evenings in there with his gadgets and electrical equipment. In the back garden, attached to the back of Jojo's annex, is a large cage for his budgerigars. I had thought budgies went out with the end of the 1950s but no – they are alive and well and giving a young man huge pleasure in north Sheffield.

I am able to believe that I did a good thing. Everyone says it was a good thing. It did what it was intended to do. It worked and it still works. For some people at least.

I began to throw stuff out. Even before I got to the point of telling Heidi she could have my house, after which there would be no going back, I began to throw stuff out. There was a lot to throw. The charity shops of North Sheffield were in for an unlooked-for increase in their stock. Much sooner than I'd ever thought I would be able to contemplate it, I was going to have to get rid of Pauline's belongings, as well as a large proportion of my own.

The suitcases came down from the top of the spare room wardrobe; the contents of them went back into the black binbags and into the boot of my car. I did not pause to look at any of them. Then I wondered why I was keeping suitcases and loaded them into the car as well. Then I thought they would be useful for transferring stuff to the bungalow and got them out of the car and began filling them with papers and school books and National Curriculum folders, and then realised that they were too heavy to lift and that I hadn't sorted any of it and there might well be stuff I could throw away into my paper recycling bin. Then I sat down and made myself a cup of tea and told myself to get a grip and start behaving in a logical fashion.

It took most of the afternoon to deal with Pauline's clothes. I took the fancy ones to a posh little shop in Hunter's Bar, where each garment had to be examined for faults and stains and processed into a book with my details. Would Pauline have preferred for them to benefit Barnado's or Age Concern? Or would she have thought a charity shop would not know what they were worth and would sell them too cheaply? This way, Heidi and the kids could benefit, and I was pretty sure she would want that. Well, it was done.

When I got home I put some of her sweaters and trousers into my drawers – which I thought I would never be able to do – and that left her everyday coats and shoes and bits and pieces to go back into the binbags, and back into the boot of the car.

I phoned Heidi, rather than tell her face to face, but when she answered I found I could not say it. Instead I told her about the dress agency and asked if

Jarvis would be free to come and help me lift some boxes.

'What are you doing?' she said.

'Just a bit of sorting,' I said. I don't think at that time the word 'decluttering' had been invented. Certainly it was not a Thing like it is now.

'Books,' I said to Jarvis. 'I've got too many and some of them I know I'm never going to read again. I need to sort through them and put anything I don't want into this box and then you will lift it into the car.'

'Ok,' he said. He looked at the heaps of paper on the dining table and on the floor. 'What about all that?'

'We'll get to that,' I said.

'Why are you getting rid of stuff?' he said.

'I'm moving house,' I said. I did not dare to look at his face.

'You haven't sold it,' he said.

'No,' I said. 'It's more like a sort of house swap.'

'What?' he said. 'Do you mean like I said? Swap this for the bungalow?'

'That's what I thought I would do,' I said. 'Would your mum agree do you think?'

I thought at this point he would leap around the room in some sort of glee or triumph, but he waited for quite a number of heartbeats before he nodded and finally said, 'I think it would help. Shall I ask her?'

'Ask her when you go home,' I said. I did not want a big drama. 'Right now, I need you up that step-ladder, handing me down that top shelf of books, one at a time.'

We, my sister and I, were never serious readers but I have never been one for throwing things away so over a lifetime I had collected a serious number of books. I would not claim to have read them all. The bookshelves Jarvis was tackling were only part of it; there were more in my bedroom, more in the box room, and small piles wherever you might look, on windowsills, behind armchairs. Most of them, I was determined were going to go; I could always get more when I wanted to.

Now, of course, the libraries and bookshops are closed, and I cannot get more unless I resort to Amazon. Although I have over the last few years acquired more books, I am missing the number and the choice I once had and did not appreciate. 'Read Middlemarch' the online forums advise; 'Read Dickens' and I would have a go but they all went in the great purge, down to the second-hand bookshop on Holme Lane, which itself is long gone. And yes I know I can buy some online, and I am fully capable, and I can afford it so why am I moaning? I know.

We found boxes, not too big because one of the things I have learned is that a box of books is heavier than a normal elderly woman can comfortably lift, and, as a first instalment, the contents of my downstairs bookshelves was put into the car.

'Can I go and tell her now?' said Jarvis.

It was only about five minutes until Heidi was on the phone, in tears, and there was no way back, for me.

'And there's no point,' I said to Adam, later, 'in doing it on a temporary basis. If we're going to move everything from here to there and your stuff in here, it might as well be for good.'

'Don't commit yourself to that,' he said. 'Let's say we'll look at the situation again once we've got Heidi's own house back again.'

'I don't want to move twice,' I said.

'I get that,' he said, 'but we don't want to do anything permanent just yet. We need to see how we get on.'

'If you say so,' I said. I knew he was being reasonable and it was making me really angry.

'We're very grateful,' he said. 'Heidi cried when she told me you'd offered. I keep looking round and finding she's in tears again.'

'She'll be fine,' I said.

It was not a straightforward job, moving their stuff from the bungalow, and from the upstairs of Heidi's own house, and Adam's belongings from his wife's house, and some of his things that were in storage, moving it all into my house which was already full of stuff which had to go to the bungalow but couldn't fit in there until they were out. Cardboard boxes, in particular, if not clearly labelled, could make the journey there and back numerous times before being opened and finding themselves in the wrong house. It took several days, during which time Jojo went to his Centre without any fuss while Heidi and I and Jarvis juggled the two little ones and packed and shifted boxes, and unpacked some and left others for later. Jojo's night terrors did not go away but somehow we pushed them aside. We were dealing with it. And it worked. As soon as he had what he wanted – sleeping in my house but with Heidi in the same house – he subsided back to his normal phlegmatic self. You would not know he had ever been disturbed.

The first night I slept in Pauline's house I worried that something would happen to upset me too. I too might go to pieces and start throwing things and disturbing the neighbours. But no. I was tired from lifting and sorting and packing, and even on a temporary camp bed I slept well and was aware of no ghosts.

And I have lived here ever since. Sometimes I even believe that I am used to it. I recognise my neighbours though I do not hold conversations with them. Until I retired from work at the age of sixty-seven the bungalow was only the place where I ate and slept. I arrived earlier at school; I stayed later and did my admin and preparation in my classroom, with the cleaner hovering round me. When I came home I ate something – not much because I would have had a school dinner of two courses – maybe watched a bit of TV, and went to bed. Weekends and holidays I went for long walks, mostly on my own. I stayed away from the Loxley Valley; I associated it so much with Pauline and that insane time after she died that I almost believed she had died in 1864, along with the Bisbys and the Spooners and the scores of others. I am still slightly deranged.

In the last three years, since I retired I have had to spend more time at home. I am able by now to use the word 'home' to signify Pauline's bungalow. I can't say that I have used the time well. In fact, the current lockdown has made next to no difference to me. I am not a social being.

I have been out of quarantine for a couple of weeks. I have been to the small local supermarket to buy groceries and chocolate. I have avoided people coming along the pavement towards me by diverting into the road – it's a sort of grown-up game of chicken: which of us will make the decision to cross to the other side. I have talked to Barbara on the phone and tried (possibly for the first time ever) to cheer her up. I have talked to Alan, often, and to Verona, though not Olive because she is too deaf. I have not told them any of the things that might worry them. I am feeling quite proud of myself.

The weather has been unbelievably warm and spring-like. Pauline's tulips, though still an affront to the eyes, are luminous in the sunshine. We are told the lockdown will continue for at least another three weeks. Three weeks before there will be any possibility of relaxing the rules. It's all the same to me.

I go to the Co-op to stock up on some essentials – doughnuts and alcohol. You have to stand in a carefully spaced queue outside and every time a customer comes out of the door a young man beckons the next person in. In front of me is a short elderly man carrying a cloth bag – what Auntie Vi would have called a spud bag, don't ask me why. I take no notice of him until he steps aside to allow a fat woman to get past and then I realise it is Trev.

'Hello Trev,' I say, and then wish I hadn't.

He seems not to know who I am, peering at me with his eyes half closed and I realise that his sight has deteriorated.

'Pam.' I say. 'Dearly.'

'Pam,' he says. 'Hello. Long time.'

'I know. Are you all right?' This is how every conversation starts these days.

'I'm well,' he says. 'Only trouble is, I broke my glasses – trod on them – and of course the opticians are closed.'

'Haven't you got a spare pair?'

'Can't find em,' he says. 'Anyway, how are you?'

'OK,' I say.

'How's the garden? Have you done – what's it called, a makeover? Done a makeover yet?'

He knows. He's looked through the side gate and seen what I have and haven't done. He's seen Pauline's garden dwindling like an old person, just fading away.

'Just started doing a bit,' I say.

'Weather's been fine for it.'

'Yes.'

'I knew,' he says, 'I knew you'd put your mark on it in the end.'

Someone else comes out of the shop and we shuffle forward.

'How's Heidi and the gang?' he says.

'All good.' I stop and think. 'Did you know Jarvis has a baby now? Little girl.'

'I heard. Must be a strange time to have a new baby, but then, they weren't to know were they. He's a good lad, your Jarvis, he'll make a nice dad. Shame Pauline isn't alive to see her.'

It's very seldom now that I hear her name, so seldom that's it's a slight shock, a feeling of What right do you have to say her name? I try to smile though, and then realise that he probably can't distinguish my expression. Then it's his turn to go into the shop.

Of course, when it's my turn I catch up with him – there he is, peering at the labels of tins, trying to guess what it is he's looking at. I try to edge past him, but he sees me.

'Is that you Pam? Is this chicken soup I've got here? I don't want mushroom, can't abide mushroom.'

I have to go closer to him than is recommended to sort out what he wants and what he's got in his basket. At his age – he must be about eighty by now - he should have someone fetching his shopping for him. I suppose I could do it, but I push the thought away. I do not wish to be responsible for another person.

'Isn't there someone who could do your shopping for you?' I say, once we've paid and got outside the shop.

'I haven't got anyone,' he says. 'No wife, no children. My sister lives in Essex –'

'So does mine,' I say, as if it has any bearing on the situation.

'– my neighbours are all elderly too. And anyway, I like to get out. It's just – without my specs I'm helpless.'

'Can they be mended? I mean if there was an optician open.'

He shrugs, as if there's no hope of that, but he says, 'The glass isn't broken. One of the lenses came out of the frame and I was trying to get it back in – you know those little screws – but I couldn't see well enough of course. Then I dropped the screw and while I was looking for it on the floor I dropped the glasses and stood on them, so one of the arms has come off as well. I feel pretty stupid I can tell you.'

'Could happen to anyone,' I say. 'If I come back with you, then you could get the bits and I could take them to Heidi. She might be able to fix it, or Adam. Or even Jojo – he's good at jobs like that and he's got younger eyes than we have.'

'But I can't find the screw,' he says despairingly.

'Adam will have one that fits,' I say. 'It's worth a try.'

'I can't let you in the flat,' he says.

'OK,' I say. 'We'll stick to the rules.'

'Never mind the rules,' he says. 'I just can't have a respectable lady popping in to see the chaos I live in. Never mind little screws – some days I can't find my shoes. Or the kettle. The remote control – that goes missing too.'

'Under a cushion,' I say. 'It's always under a cushion.'

'So it is,' he says.

I wait outside his block of flats for at least half an hour, but it matters not a bit because what else would I be doing. Looking up at the balconies I can guess which one is his from the profusion of plant pots and greenery. At last he comes out, with his poor glasses in a carrier bag marked Safeway – a shop which closed down at least fifteen years ago. This, I think, must be what being old is all about.

'When all this is over,' he says, 'I'll call round and see what you've been doing in the garden. It's too long since I've been there.'

'You won't see anything,' I say. 'It's just the same as it ever was.'

'I can't believe that,' he says. 'Not from a gardener like you.' He knows.

'Look after yourself,' I say, and walk away, past windows decorated with messages of thanks for the NHS, and childish depictions of rainbows. There hasn't been any rain for weeks now, and without rain, no rainbows.

Anyway, I pass the specs on to Heidi and she calls me the following day to tell me that they're sorted and have gone back to Trev who is very grateful. 'He kept saying how kind you'd been,' she says.

Kind, I think. Not a word that many people have used to describe me.

Looking through my front window I see a man across the road spraying the dandelions that have come up through his block paving. I don't know his name or anything about him. I don't take an interest in my neighbours. But the sight of him makes me go into the back garden and look around. If Trev did come round what would he see, now that the tulips have gone over – two straggling rose bushes, some marigolds which come up and seed themselves every year, likewise some Welsh poppies which blow in from next door, a tired-looking patch of grass, some sycamore and ash seedlings that ought to be pulled out.

I stand by the back door, on my way back in. I turn and look at the world outside. Going inside, now that I don't have to, seems perverse. I could stay out here, in the sun. I could do something else in the garden. It feels quite daring. Also, I can't think what I might do, so, after all, I go inside.

I put the kettle on. I open a tin of soup. After the soup I get through half of the malt loaf I bought, reading a book which I am not enjoying. The sun is still shining outside.

I go to the little garden shed, whose door I have not opened since probably last September when I put the mower away. I brush the cobwebs off my face. I use her old gardening coat to rub the worst of the insects and dust and sticky deposits off the tools, and then take the coat to the bin and drop it in. A part of Pauline, gone. I'm going to take this easy. I'm not so young as I was and I'm out of practice, but I know where I want to start.

I take a spade and begin at the far side of the lawn. There is, after all, no place in a garden of mine for a lawn, taking up valuable flower-growing space and demanding to be cosseted and mown regularly. I drive the spade under the first edge; I chop it so there is a neat turf. I will stack them and leave them and in a couple of years there will be a nice pile of compost for me to use.

It is hard work. I had the intention of spending the whole afternoon doing it but half an hour of it has exhausted me. The portion of lawn I have exposed is pitifully small but there is no going back. I look at the birdbath and wonder if I can move it but my first attempt proves to me that I can't. I lean the spade against the birdbath, and lean myself against it too. I hardly dare to look at what I have done; I hardly dare imagine what she would say if she knew.

I go and lie in a bath, in the belief that it will be good for me after all the bending and heaving, and wonder about taking a photo of what I've done. That's what Heidi would do, and Jarvis, and the others, record its history bit by bit, and share it. No, I think. What I will do is take a photo of it now, as it is, and then no more until I've finished. No progress reports, just a simple before and after.

I spend my evening drawing a diagram of Pauline's garden. The garden. What will be my garden. I will not have a lawn. I will not have a birdbath in the middle of my view. I'm thinking of an area of gravel, low growing plants coming through it, saxifrage and Californian poppies. I'm thinking of a compost bin – maybe Adam would have time to help me make one. I'm thinking of clematis and honeysuckle; I'm thinking of pale, creamy daffodils, and tulips in white and pale pink and dark purple.

I wonder again what Pauline would say if she knew.

The last time I was here with her was a couple of evenings before that Saturday. I called round with some excuse or other – I was just feeling a bit miserable because of the weather and the way the kids in school were already disrupting lessons by exchanging Christmas cards although it was barely December. She was sitting peacefully in her room at the back of the bungalow, with the curtains drawn shut against the rain and cold. She was sewing. Quite often she did tapestry or embroidery type things, which I could never see the point of, but that evening she was making a dress for Cassie to wear at Christmas, some sort of fairy costume, all net and sequins and shiny bits and pieces. Cassie was not the most fairy-like of children but that was not, Pauline retorted when I said it, any reason to deprive her of a pretty frock.

She was hemming the bottom of it.

'I thought you had a sewing machine,' I said.

'Of course I do,' she said. 'But I only use it for curtains and big heavy stuff. I like hand-sewing. It's restful.'

She had pinned up the hem and was sewing it with long straight stitches – tacking – like we learned in junior school. As she went she removed the pins and it was so quiet that I could hear each one drop into the box. Then she would do a proper hemming stitch and remove the tacking. No short cuts for her.

We talked about Heidi and the children as We always did. She asked me if I had met the new boyfriend yet – that would have been Gavin. She described him as a bit rough and ready but probably good-hearted. You could say that Pauline always tried to see the best in people, or you could say that she never allowed herself to look closely enough at anyone to see them in all their flawed reality. You could say she tried to kid herself.

'Think he'll last until Christmas?' I said.

'Oh,' she said, 'I expect he'll go to his mum's at Christmas. He told me he's very close to his family.'

'Did you ever,' I asked her, 'find out who is the baby's father?'

She looked at me over the top of her glasses. 'It's not actually any of our business is it?' she said. 'And I don't suppose we'd gain anything by knowing.'

'Just wondered,' I said.

We talked a little about school – staff room gossip really – and then she said, 'You seem a bit fed up. Is everything all right?'

'Not really,' I said.

'What's wrong then?'

'Oh everything.'

'Like what?'

'Well, first off, the car needs its MOT, I need to book that in and do without it for a day, and then pay some exorbitant amount for it, and I bet it'll need new tyres or something expensive. And my back door is sticking again – I suppose I'll have to get someone in but it's such a stupid little job –'

'Maybe Gavin would do it for you.'

'What does he do?'

'Something with tools, I don't know what. But he's a big strong lad, and very keen to help.'

'And the window cleaner has put a note through my door saying I owe him for the last six months. I can't help it if he calls for his money while I'm out, can I, so that's another bunch of money, and I can't even remember if he's done the windows.'

'Mm,' she said.

'And I need to get my best jacket dry-cleaned; it's got ketchup all down the front. *And* that Angie Willis is bothering me to change classrooms with her on Friday afternoon – something about sockets and wanting to use three bits of gear in one lesson.'

'You don't like her do you?'

'I don't like gathering my entire Year Nines and all their books and traipsing across the corridor, and coming back to find she's moved everything I need for the next lesson.'

'You *are* in a grumpy mood,' she said. 'What would you say if I asked you to come shopping with me on Saturday?'

'Not Christmas shopping?'

'No, not really, just ordinary shopping. Looking round the shops, see what there is. I'm not buying anything just yet but I like to have some ideas for the children. We'll have a look in John Lewis and go down The Moor. We could have lunch out. Treat ourselves.'

'I don't call shopping a treat,' I said, 'though I know you do.'

'Don't be a misery,' she said. 'I'll call for you Saturday ten o'clock. And don't pull that face. It's not going to kill you.'

And here I am digging up her garden in sunshine that is sharp and sparkling. If I look up, over the roof of the bungalow, I can see the lime trees that mark the bottom edge of my old garden, still in the process of leafing up. You can still see each leaf distinct, moving randomly in what is quite a stiff breeze, blue sky behind, like spring in a picture book for children.

So, We were in Debenhams, a few weeks before Christmas and We were arguing about Christmas presents. She loved it all, making lists and going out and finding just the perfect object, spending more money than she should, trailing round from store to store, department to department, stopping for coffee, struggling back to the car with more than she could carry. This was not my approach at all. I always gave her a present, but that was it for me. I gave money to Heidi for her to buy something for her three older kids, and I wasn't going to bother at all about the baby, because he didn't know it was Christmas, he wasn't going to expect anything. We argued about this sort of thing every year and that's what We were doing on the escalator going up to the Homeware section.

'See,' she said when we got there. 'I told you.'

There were some of those heavy iron casseroles, reduced.

'You've got at least one,' I said.

'For Heidi,' she said.

'Heidi doesn't cook,' I said. 'It will be wasted on her.'

'Well, for Olive then.'

'Don't be daft, ' I said. 'The postage on that will be massive. I bet Olive's got one already.'

'It's true,' she said, 'I don't usually spend that much on Olive. But Heidi –'

'It will sit in her cupboard for ever,' I said. 'But you do what you want.' And I walked off, not to look at anything in particular, just to see if she would follow me. When she didn't I went back over and she was still looking at them.

'Red or blue?' she said.

'You choose,' I said. 'I told you, I'm having nothing to do with it. Anyway, I thought we were here for the toy department.'

'We'll go there next,' she said.

'I'll see you up there,' I said, and took the escalator to the next floor, where I wandered round aimlessly, wondering why anyone would inflict so much noisy plastic on their children.

I did not hear anything from the direction of the escalators, but when I got tired of waiting for her and went to go back down before she started thinking about canteens of cutlery or sets of champagne glasses – well, then I noticed that the escalators had stopped and that at the bottom there was a huddle of people. I went down the stairs and looked for her and it took me several tours of the entire floor before I thought to look at where the group of people were gathered.

When I approached I could hear her voice.

'I'm fine,' she said. 'Really. I just need a hand up now.'

Two people helped her to her feet.

'I'm sorry,' she said. 'Sorry to be such a nuisance.'

'Come and sit down,' said a store employee, probably the designated first aider. 'Come to the office and let's make sure you're OK.'

'Just a bit out of breath,' said Pauline. She looked up and saw me. 'There you are. I'll be all right now,' she said to the woman. 'There's my sister.'

People began telling me what had happened and simultaneously loading me with Pauline's purchases and bags. It was clear to me that she had bought not one but two casseroles, and I gathered from the accounts of the helpful ones that she had tripped and fallen while going up the escalator.

'Good thing for her she wasn't going down,' said someone.

'Good thing for all of us,' said someone else. 'You wouldn't want one of these hurtling down on to you.'

'I'll be all right now,' she said, and smiled round at everyone as she always did, so that they would like her.

It was as soon as we got outside, me carrying these two big heavy boxes, that she said she had to sit down, and she sat down there and then, on the floor, shoppers going past us in all directions, couples and singles and people with buggies, and teenagers and everything, skirting round us as they skirted round the Jehovah's witnesses, ignoring us as they ignored the busker in the doorway of the shut down Woolworths. She was sweating and pale.

'I don't feel so good,' she said.

'What hurts?' I said.

'I don't know,' she said, faintly. 'I feel sick.'

I tried to get her up but she resisted. 'I can't.'

One of the people – a man – who had been with her in the store came through the doors and saw her there.

'All right?' he said.

'Does it look all right?' I said and she shushed me for being rude.

He walked off, but then came back with his phone in his hand and offered to call us a taxi.

'We've got a car in John Lewis car park,' I said. 'But I don't know if you can walk that far?'

Someone else had stopped and joined in. 'Ambulance,' she said. 'I mean it. She's looking not at all well.' She took me to one side and said, 'I saw it happen. She didn't fall far, she just tripped, but she went down *onto* those heavy boxes. She could have some internal injury.'

'Are you a doctor?' I said. I didn't mean it rudely.

'No,' she said. 'But if she was my friend I'd get an ambulance.'

The man with the phone stopped trying to find a taxi firm and dialled 999.

Pauline did not look any better. 'I can't stop yawning,' she said. Her face was shiny with cold sweat and she was shivering.

Time expanded and shrunk again the way it does when you've been drinking too much, and the ambulance came – quickly or eventually, I don't know which.

I saw her into it and told her I would get the car from the car park and drive after her to the hospital so that we would have it there for when she came out. I was pleased with myself for thinking it all out. She kept her handbag with her, I picked up her shopping bag containing some Playstation games for Jarvis; what happened to the casseroles I will never know.

I hurried, against the flow of people it seemed, to the car. I drove to the Northern General. I scrabbled in my bag for change to pay for the car park there, I followed the signs to A and E, I gave her name, I looked around the waiting room for her but she was not to be seen among the subdued crew nursing a bleeding head or a sprained wrist. Someone took me through to another place and someone told me things that could not be true and I saw Pauline, and she was dead.

Since then it has never left my mind, the other thing I said to her, before I went on my own up to that stupid toy department. 'Do what you like,' I said to her. 'But don't expect me to carry them.'

These days, people are buried with a minimum of ceremony, no mourners allowed. 'No goodbyes' the papers say and we are supposed to be sorry, or angry, or something, as if a funeral is something to look forward to, record on video. That is not – even now – how Pauline's funeral seems to me. I've been to funerals that I can look back on and think, Oh yes, Auntie Vi's was the one where the sun came out so suddenly as they were lowering the coffin into the grave, Vincent's was the one where a completely unknown bunch of people turned up and proved to be his bird-watching club, which none of us knew about. Pauline's is just a blur, but a painful one even after all this time. Yes I would prefer to have had to stay away.

Dearly, **Pauline June**, on 2nd December
following an accident.

Much loved sister of James, Edward, Maureen,
Barbara, Alan, Pamela and the late Vincent,
mother of Heidi and adored Granma of
Jordan, Jarvis, Cassidy and Jayden.

That notice in the paper, Barbara did that without consulting me. It was her doing, all the names, Jim and Eddie with their full Sunday names, as if we were posh. She said afterwards that she had consulted me but I knew she hadn't.

The funeral was – I can't say what it was. The people were like water swirling round me, saying things, changing places, changing faces, saying the same things, or something else, I couldn't keep up. There were people I knew, there were people I didn't know, there were people I knew very well but just couldn't place. A woman with dark red lipstick and very long fingers turned out to be, after I'd looked at her blankly, saying nothing, to be someone whose Christmas parties I'd attended for years – though under duress from Pauline.

Though I had only ever worked at that one school, Pauline had been at several – four I think – and there were people from each one, people she had kept in touch with, and they kept coming up to me, saying things about her, how nice she was, how the kids all thought she was nice, what a helpful colleague, what a good friend, what a shock, what a loss. And where was her daughter, they would say, they needed to go and tell her how much they would miss her mother.

Heidi was, as they say, in bits. So was Jarvis, and before the actual service got going I saw someone taking him away. I thought, I should have thought of that.

Our school closed for the afternoon and the kids from her class were allowed to attend – they came in quite gaily and sat all together at the back of the room and gradually went quiet and began to snivel. Lots of other kids came too, some with parents, and were milling about outside. Except Jimmy all our brothers and sisters were there, and Verona and Alison. Some nephews and nieces showed up – Bradley I remember, and Nicky who We had known well when We were children together. There were others.

It was three weeks since it had happened. We'd been lucky, people told us, to get all the technicalities dealt with that side of Christmas; we'd been lucky to get fitted in, at the busiest time for the funeral trade. It was like they were saying that Pauline was lucky – got in just in time, die the following weekend and she'd have been in her box all over Christmas, whereas now –. And at least the weather's stayed nice for it, someone said, as if it was a wedding they were at. God, people.

I had no one. All afternoon, though there were people swimming about in front of me all the time, and though the service was supposed to offer comfort and closure – and we had worked on it together, Heidi and me, in some meetings at her house with the woman she'd found on the internet who offered custom-made humanist services for all occasions – all afternoon and evening too, I had no one. I was a rock in the ocean and the waves of people broke over me and washed themselves away again. They came up to me, they said their piece, they went away to queue up to speak to Heidi, they never returned to me. I remained unaccompanied, like a tree stump where the birds don't go.

The weather alternates between cold and windy, and as warm as proper summer. No rain, which makes for harder work when getting a spade through the dry soil. I alternate between the lawn and the cutting down of overgrown bushes.

I tell Heidi what I'm doing. 'About time,' she says.

'I need bags for the rubbish,' I say. 'Though who knows when the tip will be open again.'

'We've got bags,' she says, and shortly after Jayden arrives with some of the contents of Adam's shed.

Jayden – who was at one time called 'the baby' – fourteen next week, would be choosing his options if school was open, though what options you choose when your ambition is to be a professional e-gamer I can't begin even to wonder. I've never had much to do with him. He was too young to know Pauline; he can't remember being flooded out of his house; he has never known a different father figure than Adam, the fact that he lives in what was once my house means nothing to him, even if he knows about it. He stands inside the gate and looks around at the piles of weeds and twigs and prunings, at me in my dirtiest old clothes, at the stone birdbath which is too heavy for me to move so is still in its place in the centre of what was once a lawn.

'Help me move this thing,' I say.

He looks doubtful, probably because he's been told to stay at a proper distance. 'Where do you want it?' he says.

'Anywhere,' I say. 'Over there by the shed, out of the way. I'll help you.'

'I can do it,' he says, and apparently he can, though it's more dragging than lifting.

He stands and looks at the dry clods of the churned up lawn, at the broken roots of dock and dandelion sticking out, at the deep scar he has just made by hauling the birdbath across it.

'Whose idea was this?' he says.

'Mine,' I say.

'Were you bored?'

'I suppose.'

'So what gave you the idea?' I never knew a teenager so nosey.

'I don't know,' I say. 'I just met an old friend and – it must have been something he said.'

'Oh,' says Jayden. 'Well, any time you want heavy lifting done, give us a call.'

'Thanks,' I say. 'Do you want a cup of tea?'

'Got to go,' he says, and goes.

I was ready to pack up for the day but seeing that last remaining bit to be dug, just a small patch, spurs me on to finish. I stack the last of the turves and cover them. Step one is accomplished and in spite of having had a different plan I cannot help but take a photo of it in the light of the setting sun. It is a long time since I have felt so much satisfaction.

I know what will happen. The renovation of the garden will take longer than I imagine. It will be held up by bad weather; I will not have the strength to do as much as I want to; there will be unforeseen obstacles; garden tools will break; orders for gravel or compost will fail to arrive. I will study pictures in magazines; I will change my mind about how I want it to be; I will prowl round the newly reopened garden centres and buy unsuitable plants, some of which will thrive and others of which will fail to come up next year. This time next year I will still be working on it; bits of it will have to be redone because I will have not dug deep enough into the roots of the pernicious weeds. I know all this; I have made a garden before. I am resolved not to be disheartened.

I still think 'We' and even some of the time, say 'We.' It has faded, the We-ness of life, with the passing of time, and the looks I have had when I've forgotten that I am 'I.' But I never yet have a settled feeling that 'I' is what I am. I am never without her, even after so many years.

Sometimes I feel like a motherless child. Sometimes I –

SOURCES & ACKNOWLEDGEMENTS

Geoffrey Amey (1974): *Collapse of the Dale Dyke Dam 1864*

Mick Drewery: *The Great Sheffield Flood of 1864: Inundation*

Samuel Harrison: *A Complete History of the Great Flood at Sheffield*, British Library Historical Print Editions

Peter Machan and Eric Leslie (1999): *The Dramatic Story of the Sheffield Flood*

Thanks to Alistair McLean at Weston Park Museum for meteorological information and to Sheffield Local Studies Library for being there.

ABOUT THE AUTHOR

Susan Day has been making up stories since before she could do joined up writing, but it took a while before she became brave enough to let other people read them.

Susan was brought up in Enfield and lived in Colchester, Leicester and Paisley before settling in Sheffield. She has a husband, three children and a garden a bit like Pamela's.

Also by Susan Day

WHO YOUR FRIENDS ARE

Plain Pat and Lovely Rita – childhood best friends who shared lives and confidences through the 1950s and 60s.

As the two friends follow different paths through the 70s, they grow apart, but Pat stays loyal to her friendship with Rita and her sisters.

Now, years later, Pat finds herself with time on her hands, and begins to look back on her relationship with Rita – at the same time as she has a crisis in her own life and problems in her grown up family.

A wonderful book about rites of passage – from the 1950s to the present day. Sometimes raw; often poignant; with deft dialogue and a feel for the realities of teenage friendship and subsequent family life and its unexpected twists and turns.

Robin Kent, author of *Agony Aunt Advises*

A deceptively simple story that makes you think about relationships, self-deceit and how we fail to spot the obvious.

Barbara Bannister, author of *The Tissue Veil*

THE ROADS THEY TRAVELLED

Four girls set out one wartime morning, on a day that will bind them together for years to come. Work and marriage, children and divorce, change and death.

Many years later they are still in touch, and still trying to resolve the tragedy that has been a constant in their lives. What did happen to Marcie?

Read carefully and you may recognise some of the characters from *Who Your Friends Are*.

Ordinary is made extraordinary by the intricacies shared in this beautifully woven tale of lives shaped by the forces of history... The reader is drawn into a skilfully painted picture of lives, changed forever by war.

Bryony Doran, author of *The China Bird*

Offers fresh new perspectives on lives lived – its pages are filled with moments and stories that are a pleasure to take into the imagination.

Docs and Daughters Book Group, Bristol

HOLLIN CLOUGH

CONCEALMENT: (*Verbs*) To conceal, hide, put out of sight, screen, cloak, veil, shroud, muffle, mask, disguise, camouflage.

There are families that would fall apart if the truth came out.

Jen admires her father and Frank believes that his daughters are happy, but no one in any family knows the whole story.

This family has fractured before, and been patched up by secrets and evasions.

Now things are about to change.

The more I read, the more I enjoyed it. A real page-turner – well-written and believable.

Laura Kerr, Botanical Book Group, Sheffield

A book that makes you think. Susan Day expertly tackles the relationships within families and their dynamics; her characters are very convincingly drawn and deftly written. Thoughtful and entertaining.

Steven Kay, author of *The Evergreen in Red and White*

BACK

Joan Jones leads a quiet and orderly life until she receives a postcard from an old boyfriend.

Viv feels on top of things until she becomes intrigued by the new member of her choir.

Bill is hoping for someone to love.
Road trips, crises and confusion ensue.

An enjoyable romp through some ordinary yet extraordinary lives. Full of all too believable characters whose inept communications result in missed meetings, long car journeys, petty rows and tricky situations. A look at human life which reflects both its amusing and poignant aspects. Well worth a read.

Tilly Northedge, Cobnor Book Group, Sussex

The dialogue and interplay between her characters vividly reveals them, drawing out and colouring their contrasting natures, histories and motives with little need of further description.

Brian Sellars, author of *The Whispering Bell*

Other Leaping Boy titles

THE CHILD WHO FELL FROM THE SKY
Stephan Chadwick

Untold secrets of a post-war childhood

A true story of a child born in war-torn London soon after the Second World War whose early memories are of the care and security given to him by his grandmother and a guardian angel who watches over him. At six he finds out a devastating secret that changes his life. He withdraws into his own world, searching for understanding and meaning. Isolated from his family and children of his own age he turns to his angel for love and guidance but even she cannot save him from what is to come.

'Sometimes a book can just sneak up on you and contradict your expectations and this is such a book. There is nothing flashy about it, but nor is it didactic, and it has a raw, poetic quality that to my mind puts much more scholarly writers to shame.'

Amazon review

'This is an extraordinary, raw, and powerful book.'

James Willis, author of *Friends in Low Places*

HOW TO TALK TO TEENAGERS

If you have teenagers in your life – at home, at work, or in your neighbourhood – this book may stop you tearing your hair out! It will give you insights into how teenagers tick, and strategies to get their co-operation.

➢ Explains how teenagers see the world
➢ Packed with examples from day-to-day life
➢ Focuses on what to say to get them on board
➢ Includes 'maintaining boundaries' and 'avoiding conflict'
➢ Gives tips on how to stop the nagging and shouting
➢ Encourages adults to see the positive in teenagers
➢ Concise chapter summaries for easy reference

'Lucinda has captured the art of dealing with teenagers in a fantastic, easy to use guide.'

John Keyes, Social Inclusion Manager
Arsenal Football Club

'A superb guide – the key issues and techniques of interacting with young people are covered in a practical, easy to understand way. A great introduction to working with young people. I'd recommend it to anyone.'

Mark Todd, Chief Executive
Ocean Youth Trust South

Books for children

The TOM AND JAKE Series
Helen MccGwire

Six charmingly written and illustrated little books about Tom and Jake, two small boys who live with their family and animals in an old farm-house in Devon. The stories are based on the experiences of the author's five children during the 1960s, whilst living in the countryside.

Tom and Jake
More About Tom and Jake
Tom and Jake & The Bantams
Tom in the Woods
Tom and Jake & Emily
Tom and Jake & The Storm

'Enchanting ... it takes us back to the 1960s and the adventures of the two young heroes, living in the countryside with the world to discover. Ideal for grandparents and young listeners, and a springboard for reminiscences, too. The story and prose are realistic and precise, the illustrations nostalgic and have detail for young eyes to explore and absorb. Thoroughly recommended.'

Richard Newbold, Amazon
Top 1000 Reviewer

THE VERY SKINNY WHIPPETY DOG
Kate Tomlinson
Illustrated by Sue Luxton

A beautiful picture book about a skinny whippet who finds joy playing hide and seek in the woods and fields of Devon, and contentment in the comfort of a loving home.

The delightful illustrations make this a perfect book for dog lovers, or to read to small children.

Other work by artist Sue Luxton can be viewed at www.sueluxton.com

Any of our books can be purchased online at:

www.leapingboy.com

Lightning Source UK Ltd.
Milton Keynes UK
UKHW011414200920
370223UK00002B/143